From:

Message:

Published by Christian Art Publishers
PostNet Suite # 132, Private Bag X3706, Three Rivers, 1935, South Africa

© 2023
First edition 2023

Devotions compiled from *Whispers of Hope*

Designed by Christian Art Publishers

Cover designed by Christian Art Publishers
Images used under license from Shutterstock.com

Scripture quotations marked NLT are taken from the Holy Bible, New Living Translation, copyright © 1996, 2004, 2015 by Tyndale House Foundation. Used by permission of Tyndale House Publishers, Carol Stream, Illinois 60188. All rights reserved.

Scripture quotations marked NIV are taken from the Holy Bible, New International Version®, NIV® Copyright © 1973, 1978, 1984, 2011 by Biblica, Inc.® Used by permission.
All rights reserved worldwide.

Scripture quotations marked THE MESSAGE are taken from The Message, copyright © 1993, 1994, 1995, 1996, 2000, 2001, 2002 by Eugene H. Peterson. Used by permission of NavPress.
All rights reserved.

Printed in China

ISBN 978-0-638-00051-1

© All rights reserved. No part of this book may be reproduced in any form without permission in writing from the publisher, except in the case of brief quotations in critical articles or reviews.

24 25 26 27 28 29 30 31 32 33 – 14 13 12 11 10 9 8 7 6 5

Mini Devotions

MEANINGFUL MOMENTS
with *God*

STEPHAN JOUBERT

Christian Art
PUBLISHERS

Day 1
The Right Name

"My Father's will is that everyone who looks to the Son and believes in Him shall have eternal life."
– John 6:40 NIV –

Here is an important rule for you to remember until that very moment when you take the first step on the other side, the side of death. Also remember it for the rest of eternity: When you stand face-to-face before God and He wants to know why you are there, you must appeal immediately to the only Savior in the entire universe.

Declare that you know the name of the One on whom you have built all your hope: Jesus Christ. He alone is your Lord! This simple confession will unlock the doors of eternity for you. Jesus will be there to welcome you to an everlasting feast!

What a privilege to know the most important Person in the universe by name. What an honor to have the most exclusive name of all on one's lips, to speak it with respect and love and to give it a place of honor in one's heart. You should never become used to this privilege. You should let the Spirit guide you to stand before our great God with a sense of wonder time after time. Respectfully give praise to His name in your every prayer.

Day 2

In Step with God

I will teach you wisdom's ways and lead you in straight paths. When you walk, you won't be held back; when you run, you won't stumble.

– Proverbs 4:11-12 NLT –

How do you keep pace with the rhythm of the Lord?

Make time for the Word (Psalm 1): Make time in your daily program to read God's Word. The Bible must be your daily guide. You must replenish yourself regularly with the right kind of good news.

Make time for prayer: To really hear God's voice, you have to switch off the noise around you: the TV, the radio, the phone, as well as your busy schedule. You have to put aside quiet time for sitting alone at the feet of the Lord (Matt. 6:5-6). Choose a quiet garden or a room, where noise won't disturb you, and where you are also able to silence the noise within you.

Make the right kind of friends: Instead of keeping company with people who are frivolous or devoid of any hope, you should rather spend time with people who uplift you as a person. Make a point of befriending people who can teach you to walk close to the Lord. Your role models and mentors should be people who walk the Lord's road of grace every day.

Day 3

God's Dreams

"Before I formed you in the womb I knew you."
– Jeremiah 1:5 NIV –

God dreams, and He dreams big. He dreams about a new world, one where His will prevails. He dreams about a society where hate is defeated, and injustice loses. He dreams about the poor having enough food to eat and about lonely people being cared for. He dreams about people who live together safely and who love one another. He dreams about His kingdom spreading across the earth like a runaway bushfire, and billions of people bowing before Jesus. He dreams of people who discover His treasure in the field, as Jesus tells us in Matthew 13, and then surrender everything to get hold of it.

God dreams new dreams. Here's the good news—you have a pertinent place in God's dreams. He noticed you when He dreamed big about people and His creation. He wants to use you to make His dreams a reality. You should report for duty at once. He'll take care of the rest.

The Lord will cause streams of living water to flow through you. He'll use you to touch the lives of those around you. He will give His dreams wings in and through your life. So, what are you waiting for?

Day 4

No Safe Bid

God called you to do good, even if it means suffering, just as Christ suffered for you. He is your example, and you must follow in His steps.

– 1 Peter 2:21 NLT –

Just listen to those wishes we express at the beginning of the new year or on someone's birthday. Such wishes are normally "safe." They teem with words like happiness, health, and prosperity. It's fine to express a wish that good things will happen to another person on their journey, but are these the only good things in life? Is it only in prosperity that your faith grows? Is life only about green pastures and still waters? Or isn't the deep, dark valley of Psalm 23 maybe one of God's favorite places of growth?

What about a daring challenge today? One like provocateur and author Erwin McManus signs in his books: "Risk everything!" Isn't that exactly what we need sometimes in our faith? Even more, is faith as such not a constant challenge? Isn't it the chance of a lifetime to walk with the living God? Faith asks for courage in the midst of disbelief, selfishness and opposition. As Paul tells us in Romans 8, faith asks that we must carry on hoping despite all hopelessness. It asks for boldness to walk on God's heels when you'd rather be going off in your own direction.

Day 5
Teaching Stones to Talk

This hope will not lead to disappointment. For we know how dearly God loves us, because He has given us the Holy Spirit to fill our hearts with His love.
— Romans 5:5 NLT —

Can stones talk? Yes. When? When humanity starts silencing God. That's what Jesus says when the religious leaders try to silence those who are welcoming Him to Jerusalem. Maybe we should start listening to the stones around us.

Humanity is trying to kill God's voice by silencing it, shouting louder, and looking straight past it. No wonder that we are currently experiencing what a friend of mine once called "a God-eclipse"! With our technologically advanced fire-extinguishers, we think we can extinguish God's burning bush. With our clever theories about the Bible we think we have the power and authority to do a so-called "postmortem" on the Scriptures. And then we wonder why the world is in such chaos and why we feel so alone.

Fortunately, God doesn't stop being Himself when we stop being respectful, faithful and humane. Even then He stands unchanged. Then He still allows Himself to be found by every seeker of grace. Then He removes every God-eclipse as His grace flows over and eradicates our darkness. That's why today is framed with hope.

Day 6

The Empty Tomb

"Be sure of this: I am with you always, even to the end of the age."

– Matthew 28:20 NLT –

The deceased leader of Christendom didn't lie somewhere in wake in Jerusalem while mourners walked hopelessly past. His grave is empty. Jesus is no longer to be found there. Death could not hold on to its most important victim. On the third day after His crucifixion, Jesus rose from the dead. The difference between hope and despair is the empty grave of Jesus. That's what the New Testament tells us over and over again. The resurrection of Jesus is the big difference between life and death. The empty grave is the answer to all the pain and insanity of this life. It shouts out loudly and visibly that another kind of life is possible, one filled with hope and meaning.

Now Jesus' place in heaven is filled again. He is the One before whom everyone in heaven and on earth will bow. The words of the angels at His empty grave on Good Sunday, after Jesus threw off the ties of death for good, echoes over all the earth: "He is not here. He has risen!" The last words of Jesus here on earth were that He would be with us always, until the last day (v. 20)! We are not religious orphans. He is here with us.

Day 7

In His Arms

He will order His angels to protect you wherever you go. They will hold you up with their hands so you won't even hurt your foot on a stone.
— Psalm 91:11-12 NLT —

The well-known religious reformer Martin Luther once wrote how his wife, Katharina, emerged from their bedroom one morning wearing funeral clothes, and to his question "Who has died?" she challenged him with her answer, "Your God." She explained that this could be the only reason for his gloom. Her words jerked Luther from his dark pit there and then.

David describes his own "dark pit experience" in Psalm 88. Listen to what he says: "I am counted among those who go down to the pit; I am like a man without strength. I am set apart with the dead, like the slain who lie in the grave, whom You remember no more, who are cut off from Your care. You have put me in the lowest pit, in the darkest depths" (vv. 4-6 NIV). Ouch! It is no fun to plod around in a dark pit.

Are you living in a dark pit at the moment? Look around you—even there God is at your side. He does not stand at the top watching you struggling to get out in your own strength. Hear the voice of the Lord right next to you in the dark. See Him switch on a bright light of hope right there where you are.

Day 8

One Day at a Time

Live happily with the woman you love through all the meaningless days of life that God has given you under the sun. The wife God gives you is your reward for all your earthly toil.

– Ecclesiastes 9:9 NLT –

God takes note of what you do with today's borrowed time. Don't wait for other people to make your life more enjoyable. Don't think life owes you anything. If you do you are going to sulk your life away. No, be brave! Surprise everyone. Dare to call today a day of celebration. Choose the joy of sharing some bread with friends. Put aside celebration time with your children and your spouse (vv. 8:15; 9:9). Forget about an unnecessary appointment; cancel a boring meeting. Start living, because you have only today to do it. Don't waste time. Only if it is the will of God, will you see the sun rise tomorrow. But that is still a day's journey away. In the meantime, live life to the full.

God gives life in 24 hour portions of "one day at a time." He does not guarantee the next five years of life ahead of time. At this very moment you are experiencing your own portion of abundant goodness from heaven. You are alive, not so? Your heart should be full of hope and gratitude because God has given the green light for you to be alive today.

Day 9

Who Am I?

We are God's handiwork, created in Christ Jesus.
– Ephesians 2:10 NIV –

"Who am I?" Do you ever ask yourself this question? Well, to be honest, I don't do it all that often since I made peace with the person whose body I occupy! I don't believe in introspection all that much. Years of stringent soul-searching routines, which formed part of my spiritual growth exercises, really didn't help me grow in the right direction. In the end it actually left me with more guilty feelings than ever before. It made me toxic, not healthier. It filled me with feelings of failure and doubt.

Fortunately, over the past few years I realized that I don't need to beat myself up over every negative emotion, thought or intention tucked away in the dark corners of my soul. I really found my purpose in life, namely to love Christ and serve others who cross my path. I know that I have to keep my focus on Jesus and forget about the rest.

My identity is not determined by other people's perceptions or views. I don't need to please people all the time. I only play for an audience of One. What about you? Have you sorted out your purpose in life?

Day 10

Begin Again

"All who are victorious will inherit all these blessings, and I will be their God, and they will be My children."

– Revelation 21:7 NLT –

Imagine you got the chance to start over, what would you do differently? According to research I once read, most people would like to do something differently. What a pity that the story of our lives, of which we are the main authors, very often end up as a failure. Sometimes our lives are so disordered and chaotic that we literally want to do everything over if only we had another chance.

Did you know that you really do have a chance of starting over on the Lord's terms? After all, you have the rest of the day ahead of you. It is crammed with unused hours, minutes and seconds. You have a choice—whether you are going to seize it and make the best of it to glorify the Lord, or allow the rest of the day to slip through your fingers.

Don't let today be just another 24 hours of the week. Start by making a few small changes, then progress from there.

You and I don't have to change the whole world today. We simply have to be a living blessing in the name of Jesus to those who cross our paths. That is all.

DAY 11

Trust God

Trust in the LORD with all your heart; do not depend on your own understanding. Seek His will in all you do, and He will show you which path to take.
– Proverbs 3:5-6 NLT –

It's not uncommon for us to be overly protective of those who are close to us. As parents we want to protect our kids from the rough edges of life. We also like to go the extra mile for our close family and friends. However, we can't always be physically there for each other. And it's surely not always the wisest thing on earth to try and keep our loved ones away from the adventures of life, even though life is full of dangers, challenges, and surprises. Sadly, life doesn't happen on some cloud, but right here in the real world fraught with danger. This side of the grave, life isn't perfect.

Maybe our calling is rather to pray for those we love while they are living in the danger zones of life, rather than to keep them hidden. We should rather keep their names in front of our heavenly Father.

We should trust God with their lives, and pray that He keeps them safe and on the right path. We need to trust the Father to guide us and our loved ones in life and death.

Day 12

God Is in Control

We know that God causes everything to work together for the good of those who love God and are called according to His purpose for them.

– Romans 8:28 NLT –

A few years ago, Lloyd's Bank of London tried to determine what happens to all the paperclips in their bank. Of the approximate 100,000 in use then, close to 25,000 ended up in vacuum cleaners or were thrown away; 14,163 were broken from excessive bending during telephone conversations; 4,434 were used for scratching ears or cleaning teeth; and only 20,286 were used as paperclips. In short, even the simplest of items—like paperclips invented by Samuel B. Fay in 1867—are used in ways other than intended.

It seems to me that if we can't even control the use of paperclips, we will far less likely be able to control each other or the flow of life. Maybe it was never our calling to do so. The secret of life is simply to love God and each other. And to find daily joy in simplicity, as Ecclesiastes teaches us. That's why God's invitation to us is to eat our food with pleasure and create joy before God with daily portions of simplicity. When we stop trying to control everyone and start trusting God to provide for us in His way, we make joy a welcome expectation in our lives.

DAY 13

Too Much Weight

Blessed are those who trust in the LORD, and have made the LORD their hope and confidence.
– Jeremiah 17:7 NLT –

"People say..." Isn't it remarkable how often you hear this? The opinions of "others" far too often determine what we think. Far too many churches and businesses are managed because of the opinions of others. Comments like "what would the church members say?" or "the opinions of our customers count the most!" are well-known expressions in these circles. People have to be kept happy at all costs otherwise they might withdraw their loyalty from us. But wait...do you really want to be a lifelong victim of other people's opinions? Do "they" have to keep you hostage? Is that really what the Lord expects of you? Should you work hard to win the favor of others, like some Christians think, or should you trust God to confirm your integrity in front of others in His own way?

If you constantly live for the approval of others, you're a victim. There's a better alternative. Strive only for God's approval. Put His kingdom first. Ensure that His approval motivates you. Try to receive the best compliment ever from the Lord one day: "Well done, good and faithful servant." Then you'll be free of "their opinions."

Day 14
While We're Sleeping

*In peace I will lie down and sleep, for You alone,
Lord, make me dwell in safety.*

– Psalm 4:8 NIV –

Your faith does not only happen when you're awake. Put differently, your trust in God ought to have a direct influence on how you sleep every night. The psalmist tells us in Psalm 3 that he lies down in peace and falls asleep instantly, even when a thousand people are storming toward him. He knows his life is permanently in God's hands, even when he closes his eyes at night. He knows God does not sleep, as Psalm 121 tells us. God is never off duty—never! He is awake 24/7 and 365 days of the year.

When you and I are in dreamland, God is wide awake. That's why we can trust Him with our lives and those of our loved ones when we close our tired eyes at night.

We are always in the hands of the living Lord. Therefore, we can lie down in peace, even though the land is on fire. We can even trust God, in the words of Psalm 127:3, to give us what we need while we are sleeping every single night!

Day 15
Out of Control

"You will call on Me and come and pray to Me, and I will listen to you. You will seek Me and find Me when you seek Me with all your heart."
– Jeremiah 29:12-13 NIV –

Sometimes my prayers are nothing more than pious presentations to God of my plans. Actually, they are disguised (or undisguised) instructions, together with all the necessary requests about precisely how and when it should happen. In fact, I am often so busy communicating my own needs to God that I forget to seek His presence unconditionally. I try, way too often, to stay in control of things, specifically through my prayers. That's a mistake! The essence of true prayer is being out of control. It means trusting God with everything. It means confessing that everything that I am and everything that I have, comes from Him.

God, and God alone, is in charge of my life. True prayer means becoming devoid of myself. My prayers should never be disguised attempts to regulate God's calendar and activities or to fill up His day with my selfish trivialities. For this reason, I submit myself, in childish belief and trust, to the will of God. For this reason, I kneel without any conditions before God, dependent and full of wonder. From now on, that is how I will live, dependent on my Father's grace!

Day 16
A Carefree Life

Always be full of joy in the Lord. I say it again—rejoice!

– Philippians 4:4 NLT –

Learn from a few important lessons from Jesus' favorite people. I refer to children, of course. Learn how to play and relax. Learn not to take yourself too seriously. Think of yourself as a child in a grown-up's body. Make time to laugh and play every day, to be careless, fun-loving and expressive. Share humorous stories. Laugh. It will add many joyful years to your life as well as life to your years.

Wouldn't it be a wonderful thing if joy, playfulness, rest and relaxation were a constant part of your life for the rest of the year? Your quality of life will change dramatically when you deliberately choose to celebrate life in the presence of our good Lord. Your relationship with Christ and others will look quite different if each of these relationships is surrounded by joy and happiness. You will discover the Lord in surprising new ways when you begin to trust Him with everything in a childlike fashion.

When you get into the rhythm of choosing day after day to live a carefree life, divine joy will be something you experience every day.

DAY 17

In His Hands

The LORD directs the steps of the godly. He delights in every detail of their lives. Though they stumble, they will never fall, for the LORD holds them by the hand.

– Psalm 37:23-24 NLT –

At this very moment earth is traveling through space at more than 65,000 miles per hour, while today it will complete approximately 1,4 million miles of its annual journey around the sun. At the same time earth is rotating around its own axle at an astonishing 994 miles per hour. Staggering, isn't it! It is amazing to think that God maintains everything perfectly day after day. He is the Creator of the universe, but also the Maintainer of the mighty and beautiful works of His hands. Therefore you can trust God with great things.

Nothing is ever too big for Him. He balances our world with everyone on it and everything in it. But nothing is ever too small for Him either. The detail of your life is really of interest to Him.

Take all your needs to Him today in prayer. Do so in the name of Jesus. He hears you. He sees you. He cares so much about you. The God of power is also the God of the detail of your life. Small is never too insignificant for Him, just as nothing is ever too big.

Day 18

Sleep

"I will refresh the weary and satisfy the faint."
– Jeremiah 31:25 NIV –

Someone once told me how a pastor threw his Bible at someone who had fallen asleep in his church. "If you don't want to hear the Word at least you will feel it," he added. Maybe it was only a joke.

Sleep, in fact, is a very important part of our lives. Do you sleep well? Or do your problems make you toss and turn at night? If so, the time has come for your faith in the Lord Jesus Christ to have a direct impact on your sleeping patterns.

Listen to what David says about this: "I lie down and sleep; I wake again, because the Lord sustains me" (Ps. 3:5 NIV). Rather gripping, isn't it? Trust in the Lord to deal with all your problems for a change. Then they will no longer keep you awake at night. Then you will fall asleep in the arms of the Almighty God every time.

You will no longer wake from fitful sleep in the morning; you will wake refreshed and invigorated.

Day 19
Making a Difference

"'Not by might nor by power, but by My Spirit,' says the LORD Almighty."

– Zechariah 4:6 NIV –

Recently I learned that six out of every 10 people in Africa live under the breadline. And prices of basic necessities continue to rise. Living under the breadline means those less fortunate than ourselves have to try and survive with less than $1 per day.

Jesus teaches me that I cannot look the other way when people around me are suffering. I cannot lessen the plight of the entire world, but I can ensure that at least one other person smiles due to the mercy of God flowing through me. I can pray for one person. I can visit or phone one person. I can be a soft pillow for one other person. I can give one person's dignity back. I can make time to ask one person how they are doing and really listen to what they have to say.

While you trust the Man from Nazareth with your life every day, He wants to entrust the needs of at least one other person to you. Are you ready? Can He trust you with one person? Or is your faith still a private matter?

Day 20

His Yoke

Carefully build yourselves up in this most holy faith by praying in the Holy Spirit, staying right at the center of God's love, keeping your arms open and outstretched, ready for the mercy of our Master, Jesus Christ. This is the unending life, the real life!
– Jude 20-21 The Message –

Are feelings of hopelessness and worry your best friends at the moment? Well, then, you are keeping the wrong company! They are going to rob you of your happiness, and of your faith. Resign from this hopeless brigade. Write a letter of resignation in which you declare that from now on you are not going to let any negative feelings or worries into your heart. If you give free entry to these feelings one more day, they are going to rob you of your faith eventually.

In the parable of the sower in Matthew 13, Jesus warns that worry is a big robber of faith. Be warned: The more you worry, the weaker your faith will be. On the other hand, the greater your faith in God, the more you trust in Him. His shoulders are broad enough to carry the cares of the whole world and to provide for everyone's needs. There is no reason why He will not carry yours. He was prepared to give up His Son to die for you, so why would He not care about every small detail of your life? Believe it.

Day 21

God's Hope

Let us hold unswervingly to the hope we profess, for He who promised is faithful.

– Hebrews 10:23 NIV –

Many of us read leadership books by well-known business gurus, or attend their seminars, as if their best-sellers automatically turn them into the ideal role models to follow. Do we really think that they, or the big companies of this world, get it right all the time? Don't get me wrong, I don't have a problem with listening to leadership specialists or reading their books as such, but to think they have all the answers, while we in church still don't get it, is a huge mistake.

Perhaps the biggest mistake is to still use these dated categories; those "we-they," or "church-business" categorizations. Secondly, many local churches are not doing too badly. Christ is faithful. After 2,000 years He still looks after His interests here on earth…including all local churches who follow the Jesus way. No, Jesus did not give up on His people.

Through the work of the Spirit, He is in our midst. He cares for us. He listens to our prayers. He helps us out in our hour of need. He works through us in so many beautiful ways. That's why the church offers real hope to the world.

Day 22

Fire on Your Tongue

Watch your words and hold your tongue; you'll save yourself a lot of grief.

– Proverbs 21:23 The Message –

Language is alive. The book of Proverbs says that our words are like knife stabs. Or like fine silver. Just consider how powerfully a phrase like "I appreciate you" can influence the life of another. Or a sentence, like "you are special!" On the other hand, sharp words can deeply hurt others. Hard words are dangerous. That's why the Bible says that we must carefully weigh our words and calculate their weight before they finally leave our mouths. We need to ruminate on our words twice before they leave our mouths.

Once spoken, words take on a life of their own. Therefore, ask the Lord to dip your words in pure gold before they escape from your mouth. Ask Him to change your words into medicine instead of life-threatening weapons that bruise others. Ask Him to touch your tongue like He did Isaiah's. Do you remember that when Isaiah told God that his lips were unclean, there was a coal taken from the heavenly altar to touch his tongue? His mouth was immediately purified with heavenly fire. After that, Isaiah could speak God-honoring language and share words of hope and life with others.

Day 23

Victory Tomorrow

"I have told you these things, so that in Me you may have peace. In this world you will have trouble. But take heart! I have overcome the world."

– John 16:33 NIV –

If tomorrow looks dark, today is cast in shadows. If the future feels uncertain, the present is a bad place to be. Unfortunately, many believers also feel like this about the future. That's why they look just as despondent. They stare themselves blind against that future that the media, the economy, and politicians hold up in front of them, not to mention that never-ending choir of hopeless individuals who constantly share the latest round of bad news with everyone in range.

How about a piece of truly good news? Well, here it is: God has sorted out the future already. It is not classified information that the future belongs exclusively to the Lord. Just read what the final scoreboard says in Revelation 20-22: THE LORD WINS! Nothing and nobody can prevent Him from reaching His goal. God is full speed underway to let His new heaven and new earth dawn. Know every day afresh that the Lord will win.

Never forget that Christ awaits you at the end of your own journey with a heavenly crown of righteousness in His hand (2 Tim. 4:7-8).

Day 24

Cease-Fire

He Himself is our peace, who has made the two groups one and has destroyed the barrier, the dividing wall of hostility.

– Ephesians 2:14 NIV –

The peace of Christ proclaims that there is no more enmity between heaven and earth. His death and resurrection constitute the cease-fire that connects God and us. There is no other road to God. Only Jesus brings true peace and can guarantee that it will last. The peace of Christ gives the receiver permanent access to God. If we follow Jesus' road of peace, we are assured of a place at the throne of God.

Read what Paul says in Romans 5:1-2 (NIV): "Therefore, since we have been justified through faith, we have peace with God through our Lord Jesus Christ, through whom we have gained access by faith into this grace in which we now stand. And we boast in the hope of the glory of God."

There is no more punishment from God. Peace = good news. This means that there is no condemnation for those who are in Christ Jesus (Rom. 8:1). The peace of Jesus brings about peace between people on earth who fight with one another.

DAY 25

Living the Plan

"I know the plans I have for you," declares the LORD, "plans to prosper you and not to harm you, plans to give you hope and a future."

– Jeremiah 29:11 NIV –

When you bow before Jesus, every story of your life with a bad beginning and a dreary end is wiped out! Then you become part of a brand-new story, the master-story of God! All of a sudden, your yesterdays, todays and tomorrows are fresh and new, and eternal new life unfolds before your eyes. Yes, the complete story of your life is rewritten by only One Man.

Do you know that suddenly there will no longer be a single report in heaven containing damning evidence about your sins of yesterday, no mark of the hurt you caused a loved one or of any other personal tragedy in your life? Your name is entered only once in the books of heaven and that is in the Book of Life. It has been written in the blood of Christ. Believe it. See it. Experience it. Live it!

Jesus transforms sinners into new people, into children of God. He prepares a new road for everyone who holds on to Him as their Lord and Savior. May you once again behold Jesus, the One who changes the destiny of all forever.

DAY 26

Carpe Diem

*Satisfy us in the morning with Your unfailing love,
that we may sing for joy and be glad all our days.*
– Psalm 90:14 NIV –

God likes today so much that He made it. He made it especially for us to fully enjoy! He planned it and it arrived just in time! It's only as a result of His grace that today has been added to the world's calendar. God wants us to experience today in all its splendor and beauty. We should not save our energy for tomorrow. Tomorrow is still far away.

Do not do what Shirley Valentine did when she said, "I got lost in unused time!" It is terrible to get lost in that way. Too many people are lost in time. They keep waiting for better days, instead of creating something today, in God's name!

For a change, pitch up at the most important day in your own life—today! Today has the right spiritual DNA, because it was uniquely created by God. And He gave it to the occupants of this world, including you. Don't pack today away in the cupboard of so many other wasted, unlived days. Your daily portion of heavenly bliss awaits. Consume it and live today!

Day 27
More Than a Spectator

Live a life filled with love, following the example of Christ. He loved us and offered Himself as a sacrifice for us, a pleasing aroma to God.
– Ephesians 5:2 NLT –

You should do something special with the portion of life God has lent you today. Remember that you receive life only one day at a time. You don't know if you will still be here tomorrow. You are fortunate to have received today as a gift from heaven. Do something special with it. Live and use each and every second of these 24 hours to the glory of God.

Do not let worries or problems spoil your day. Erase each concern from your mind with a prayer right away. Do not allow the wrong people to pull you down into their sinful way of life. Speak only words of encouragement when others around you make nasty remarks. Share a friendly word with a colleague at work who has become a victim of grumpiness. Send an encouraging text message to a friend whom you haven't seen in a long time. Pray for someone who the Lord has placed in your thoughts.

Do not be a passive spectator of life. Play only on the playing field of the Lord today. Live with hope. Realize once more that you are the Lord's prized possession. Jesus Christ bought you with His precious blood.

Day 28

First Aid

He has removed our sins as far from us as the east is from the west.

– Psalm 103:12 NLT –

When sin makes you stumble, do not give up and lie down in the mess. That is exactly where the enemy wants you: wounded and without hope! No, if you have stumbled, do the following:

Confess your sin: Remember the words of 1 John 1:8-2:2 that tell us that if we confess our sins, God is faithful and just and will forgive us. His Son, Jesus Christ, is our only Advocate and Intercessor at times like these.

Accept the redemption of God: When you commit sin you must immediately confess it before God in Christ. At the same time you must know that Jesus will expiate your sins. In turn, God is a righteous Judge; He will redeem you because the sacrifice of His Son is sufficient for you and all others who approach Him with their failures and sins.

Report for duty immediately: If you place your sin in all sincerity at the feet of God, you can and must know He will grant you His divine grace for the sake of Christ. Accept His special redemption and report for duty back at the front line again.

Day 29

One by One

Never tire of doing what is good.
– 2 Thessalonians 3:13 NIV –

The right kind of impact in the world occurs at the rate of one person, one word and one action at a time. Real change is not necessarily brought about by great actions and programs. When the life of one person is filled with hope because of her or his contact with me, another brand-new row of bricks is laid on the road to heaven. The territory taken up by despair, death and hopelessness decreases by one person.

When my words and deeds bring hope to the broken and when my simple actions of compassion help heal their wounds, the world suddenly becomes more bearable, humane and safe! The sunbeams of the gospel warm our world anew.

While our world is becoming colder and more impersonal, I must be the living difference for the Lord. Everyone who comes into contact with me should have my fingerprint of compassion on their lives to show for it. Others should feel and hear the clear echo of heavenly grace in my life. One by one they should move closer to hear more about God, because my life is such a powerful reflection of His love (Matt. 5).

Day 30
Don't Get Stuck

The world is unprincipled. It's dog-eat-dog out there! The world doesn't fight fair. But we don't live or fight our battles that way—never have and never will.
– 2 Corinthians 10:3-4 The Message –

If you are held hostage by negative thoughts, do what Paul recommends in 2 Corinthians. Take every negative thought captive that threatens to invade your thinking. Do it in the name of Christ immediately. Deliver that thought to Him and let Him deal with it. Give all other destructive thoughts to God as soon as you realize they are gathering in your heart. Be on the lookout for unwelcome thoughts that don't get caught up in hate, bitterness, lust, hopelessness, and other destructive things. Notice them in advance and stop them in the name of Christ.

Remember that no temptation that is too strong for you will ever come across your path. The Bible says this in 1 Corinthians 10:14. God never allows you to have tempting thoughts that you cannot say no to. Know that every temptation that comes across your path has been assessed in heaven before it reaches you. Therefore you can say no. You can resist every temptation in the name of Christ. Neither you nor any child of God has any excuse to succumb to temptation.

Day 31

Choose Joy

Whatever you do or say, do it as a representative of the Lord Jesus, giving thanks through Him to God the Father.

– Colossians 3:17 NLT –

Maybe the problem with our plans and visions is that we set challenges that are too difficult for ourselves. We want to achieve the impossible. But then our spirit is broken before we have even started. Maybe we should set smaller, more realistic goals for ourselves. And the goals should also be enjoyable! This month choose to do something with your life that will make your life and the lives of those around you happier. Choose goals which reflect God's greatness through the ordinary things you do every day (Col. 3:17).

What about the simple decision to laugh out loud at least once a day? Or to drink coffee with someone once a week? Is it too much to ask to pray for another person every day? Or to phone someone who is suffering once a week to say that you are thinking of them? Or to secretly give extra money to somebody in need? Scatter joy everywhere you go, God's type of joy.

You can't change the whole world and you don't have to. But you can make your own piece of the world a happier place. The choice is yours.

Day 32
The Joy of Life

"Come to Me, all you who are weary and burdened, and I will give you rest."

– Matthew 11:28 NIV –

One of the reasons for our rushed lives could be our desire for more earthly possessions. We exhaust ourselves in order to afford a new car, a house, a holiday, furniture, the children's education...We worry today about the problems and expenses of tomorrow.

But listen to this: God measures out grace only "one day at a time" (Matt. 6:11). He provides in all our needs—one day at a time. But when we appoint ourselves as the architects and owner-builders of our plans, that is when our faith diminishes while the speed at which we live increases by the day, so much so that we begin to devise plans to get even more unnecessary food on the table.

The solution is to hand over full control of the building plans of our lives to God. He should be the only architect of our life's house. Then we will move forward in the right direction, one day at a time. We will no longer have unnecessary man-made building plans in our lives that sap our energy and swallow our faith. Peace and simplicity will become the most precious possessions we have—gifts bestowed upon us by the Lord!

DAY 33

On Your Doorstep

Let the morning bring me word of Your unfailing love, for I have put my trust in You. Show me the way I should go, for to You I entrust my life.

– Psalm 143:8 NIV –

"A person can do nothing better than to eat and drink and find satisfaction in their own toil. This too, I see, is from the hand of God" (Eccles. 2:24 NIV). You will find true happiness when you break bread with those who are close to you. The cup of your life will run over with joy when you spend happy times with family and friends.

The true joy of living awaits you on your doorstep each day. All you have to do is to make each time you break bread or visit with friends and family a festive occasion. Treat everyone sharing your meal as a special guest. Each one has come into your life to lighten your burdens and to ease your way.

If you are far from your loved ones today, take a lesson from the early Christians. They reserved a seat for the living Lord at their communion table. Why don't you do that? Invite the Lord to be the Guest at your table, even if you're only having a simple piece of bread. There is no doubt that He will accept your invitation to celebrate with you! He is sure to free you from your feelings of loneliness today.

Day 34

True Joy

"The joy of the Lord is your strength!"
– Nehemiah 8:10 NLT –

Where do you find true and life-changing joy? Can you find it in a checkbook where you can write a whole lot of zeros? Can you find it in a brand-new house? Or maybe in that dream holiday? How about a great new job opportunity? Yes, you will surely find some joy in all these things. Such things can also be blessings directly from our heavenly Father. On the other hand, all holidays come to an end, and a house ages with time.

Where do you encounter joy that is like a constant river that provides water throughout the year; the kind of joy that is not dependent on favorable external circumstances alone? Well, Jesus offers that kind of joy. He invites us to come to Him and get it for ourselves. Joy is the gift Jesus gives to His people. Go and claim your portion today. Don't hastily put it away in one of the drawers of life. Use your heavenly joy.

You can receive it every day! Every morning an updated portion of heavenly joy awaits you with your name and address on it.

DAY 35

Your Facial Muscles

A cheerful heart brings a smile to your face.
– Proverbs 15:13 THE MESSAGE –

I heard about a boy once who found a dried leaf in his mother's Bible and asked her: "Mom, is this the fig leaf that Adam used in the Garden when he wanted to hide his nakedness?" Cute, not so? We should have more humor in our lives, don't you think? We should make more time for laughing and being jolly. Do we not serve a God of joy? In His kingdom joy wins. In His presence there is no place for sulking and pulling a long face (Rom. 14:17). Perhaps we shouldn't take ourselves and others so seriously.

Perhaps we should be more light-hearted about life (not that we should be frivolous!). A believer once made the remark that "God must have a very good sense of humor since He made human beings like us!" Whenever you are about to fly off the handle, ask yourself if it is really worth getting upset about. Try laughing out loud at yourself and others (or rather with others!) for a change.

God gave you many facial muscles, most of which get absolutely no exercise if you don't laugh. So, what are you waiting for?

Day 36

Source of Joy

"Are you tired? Worn out? Burned out on religion? Come to Me. Get away with Me and you'll recover your life. Walk with Me and work with Me—watch how I do it. Learn the unforced rhythms of grace."
– Matthew 11:28-29 The Message –

Where can you find lasting joy? Yes, surely joy can be found in everyday things, but it is only temporary. So where can you find the kind of joy that lasts? Jesus promises to give lasting joy and He invites us in Matthew 11 to come to Him and experience it. His yoke is easy to carry, for He took our burdens on His shoulders when He died for us on the cross.

Too often, religious people give the impression that they are shouldering the burdens of the whole world. It shouldn't be like that. That is not what religion is about. It is about joy. How can one find the joy of Jesus? Simply by accepting gratefully the joy that He provides. And by using it and putting it to work. All you have to do is to collect your portion of heavenly joy each morning. Ask the Lord each day that you may experience His peace, and your request will be granted instantly.

The Father's heavenly joy can never be used up—He renews it day by day!

DAY 37

Being a Worrywart

*Satisfy us in the morning with Your unfailing love,
that we may sing for joy and be glad all our days.*
– Psalm 90:14 NIV –

Simplicity is one of the joys of life. It's true, isn't it? There is joy in the simple act of breaking bread with a good friend or family member. Simple joy is playing with your children or spending time with your family. And what a joy it is to thank the Lord for the blessing of each new day. Simplicity is being satisfied. It is saying the words of Psalm 23:1 (NLT): "The LORD is my Shepherd; I have all that I need."

What are you short on? Money? A better car? Different job conditions? Well, if you worry about things you lack, you will probably always be dissatisfied with what you have. Even a new car will not be enough. You will be satisfied only when you have one with a sunroof and leather seats. Or when your new training bike looks like your neighbor's.

If you worry about things you don't have, you will always want more or something different. You will always be short of something. But if you know the Lord as your Shepherd, you will truly lack nothing. You will have as much as you need.

Day 38

Leave Haste Behind

A day is like a thousand years to the Lord, and a thousand years is like a day.

– 2 Peter 3:8 NLT –

Being hasty is a human characteristic, not a divine one. I refer to haste. God always has time. He is never in a hurry on His way to His next appointment. Take a look at the life Jesus led on earth. He always had time, even in the face of death. When His friend Lazarus died (John 11), He was still on time! He wants us to exchange our hurried, high-octane hearts for tranquil hearts.

We should have the courage to spend time walking with God in His garden. We should once again bring His garden back to life outside the gates of Paradise. God still has so many secrets He wants to share with us here on earth; so many new joys. But then we have to take action against our hurried lives. How? Well, we have to receive medicine from the Lord for that "hurry sickness" we suffer from.

This is an illness that poisons our entire existence. Haste steals our joy. It robs us of our loved ones and of everyone that matters in our lives. What for? Only so that we can say we are the latest winners of the rat race floating trophy?

Day 39
The Guest of Honor

Blessed are those who are generous, because they feed the poor.

– Proverbs 22:9 NLT –

Food is a concrete part of our faith. That's why most feasts in the Bible had to do with food and eating. Whenever the Israelites celebrated in the presence of God, they ate. The "get-togethers" of the early Christians were also characterized by simple meals. Our communion is a faint representation of the early Church's festive meals. Food, joy and faith go hand-in-hand. The first Christians recognized this as important. That's why they enjoyed eating together, despite the persecution and opposition they encountered. They invited the risen Lord as a Guest of Honor to every meal.

It's sad that we're still struggling to find the proper connection between our faith and food. Could that be because food just isn't "spiritual" enough for most of us? Go and learn from the first Christians and from other believers, like the writer of Ecclesiastes who found joy in the simplicity of bread and wine. Eat your bread with joy every day. Declare every meal spontaneously a feast.

DAY 40

Is Jesus a Hobby?

Humility is the fear of the LORD; its wages are riches and honor and life.

– Proverbs 22:4 NIV –

Jesus has become a hobby for far too many people. Whenever they show up at His "place" on Sundays He must entertain them with good sermons and fine worship music. Sadly, Jesus must make people feel good all the time. That is His job description according to many. Apparently He is there to serve the selfish needs of people. Well, Jesus is not for sale, like a toy on the shelf of any store. You do not play around with Him and decide at your own leisure when and how you will allow Him into your life. He is the Son of God. He is the Messiah, not little Jesus, the meek and mild toy for those bored, selfish, egotistic, me-myself-and-I "Christian" types.

Read the stern warnings in Jesus' own words before you decide to walk with Him: death, rejection, disappointment, a cross, far more questions than answers, suffering, joy, a strange happiness, true service...these experiences will become your companions on the road with Jesus. He will lead you on new routes. He will also let you discover old and new treasures in his Father's house that will fill you with a strange new joy, but then on His terms alone.

DAY 41

A Mere Observer

Share each other's burdens, and in this way obey the law of Christ.

– Galatians 6:2 NLT –

Are you suffering under the yoke of life's innumerous heavy burdens? Are despair and fear your closest companions? If so, you should really do something about it. "What?" you ask. Well, resign from and banish those negative emotions. Do it right away! Don't allow fear or despair to reside illegally in your heart. Also, refuse to allow a difficult work environment, loneliness or poverty to steal your freedom in Christ. Refuse to let illness and other calamities steer you off God's course.

You must do something special with this part of life that has been "lent" to you. Remember that you only have one life. Use it with wisdom! Live every aspect of it exclusively for God. Use kind words that express God's mercy to give hope to the people around you. Talk in uplifting terms when your colleagues use trite, negative or depressing language. Share a friendly smile with somebody at work, or send a supportive text message to a friend. Don't be a passive observer of life. Play on God's playing fields with love and service. Make a real difference. God's sunbeams will suddenly shine again.

Day 42
The Connecting Line

To the only God our Savior be glory, majesty, power and authority, through Jesus Christ our Lord, before all ages, now and forevermore! Amen.

– Jude 25 NIV –

On most gravestones there are two dates—a date of birth and a date of death. They are connected by a short line. That short line is known as life! What happens between your date of birth and date of death is actually what your life is all about. You don't have any control over those two dates in your life, but you do have control over your life in between them. You control where it leads—to God's city or to the city of death! Most people will not remember the dates on which your life started and ended, but they will remember the life you lived in between.

So, what are you doing with your life? Are you living a life that is worthy of imitation? Are you creating happy memories in the hearts of others? Are you leaving footprints that others can follow and that will lead them to God? Do your fingerprints bring hope and joy to people's lives? Then people will not just remember you with compassion, God will also know you well. And even better, then your real life will start, on the other side of the second date on the gravestone!

Day 43

Strange but True

No prophecy in Scripture ever came from the prophet's own understanding, or from human initiative. No, those prophets were moved by the Holy Spirit, and they spoke from God.

– 2 Peter 1:20-21 NLT –

Some believers like to define their roles in God's service in terms of the prophets of the Old Testament. Strangely, they usually only use the stories of the prophets. The real day-to-day lives of the prophets never get much attention when these believers begin to define their calling or the nature of their ministries. However, to be a prophet in the tradition of a Jeremiah, Micah or Nahum, is to live against the grain. The true prophets of Israel lived on the fringes of society. They weren't the religious flavors of the day. Prophets never formed part of the mainstream religion.

To be a prophet is to see what others don't always see, to hear what others don't usually hear. But God's prophets don't just see and hear His new future; they also make known what they heard, saw and experienced. Prophets always communicate God's new day in the Kingdom. They reveal God's heart. They are figures of hope with a new message of restoration. No wonder they vigorously challenge all systems, institutions, individuals, and groups that stand in the way of God's plans.

Day 44

Carrying the Cross

Be completely humble and gentle; be patient, bearing with one another in love.

– Ephesians 4:2 NIV –

In between all the reasons for complaining about how bad life is, you and I can choose to find our joy elsewhere. Following Jesus means having hope. Bearing His cross means being a living blessing to others.

Every day that we enjoy the privilege of living and breathing, we have the chance and honor to bear the cross of Jesus. And who knows, you and I may be the only "Bible" available to someone who finds themselves in a place of despondency. What about a gentle word of hope for them, or maybe a piece of bread to make their plight more bearable? How about a quiet prayer for a friend who is currently experiencing the sharp edge of life?

Let us carry the cross of Jesus that offers life and hope to those around us. When others start tasting and seeing life because the cross of Jesus is resting on our own shoulders, we eventually hardly even feel the weight of it anymore. The cross is only a burden when we get caught up in self-pity, or when we are not a living blessing to others.

Day 45

Real and Relevant

Having hope will give you courage. You will be protected and will rest in safety.

– Job 11:18 NLT –

I once heard about a few residents at a retirement home whose only income was a meager government pension. They did not have proper food to eat. Consequently, our church committee decided in faith to pay for the meals of 20 of these pensioners for the next year. I was moved to tears that all those serving on the committee were personally prepared to help people they didn't even know.

A week or two later I received a precious note from a lady who had been one of my teachers years ago. She wrote to say that she was in her seventies and saw for the first time how real and relevant the church can be, after hearing about our involvement with these elderly people who were suffering so much. And I know she is a very dedicated church member.

How can faith be practiced so sparsely in the church? We constantly hear the most beautiful sermons about faith, not to mention all the Bible studies on this topic. But where does the average Christian ever see faith in action? And even more importantly: where do they practice their faith? What story does your life tell today that will fill other people with hope?

Day 46

A Sharp Tongue

The more talk, the less truth; the wise measure their words.

– Proverbs 10:19 THE MESSAGE –

There is the saying "From your mouth to God's ears."

What this means is that what we say can become a self-fulfilling prophecy. Whether positive or negative, words are given life once they leave our mouths.

"If you do not have anything positive to say, rather say nothing at all." These are wise words, ones we would do well to heed if we are to reflect Jesus in our own lives.

Do you remember when Isaiah told the Lord that his lips were unclean and that his words did not glorify God, a burning coal was taken from the heavenly altar and touched his mouth? His mouth was cleansed with heavenly fire.

After that he could openly share words of hope and life with others. Let your tongue also be touched by heavenly fire!

Day 47

An Original

O Lord, You have examined my heart and know everything about me. You know when I sit down or stand up. You know my thoughts even when I'm far away.

– Psalm 139:1-2 NLT –

The Lord wants you to be yourself. He really doesn't want you to be someone else, because then you would have been that other person. Someone once said that when he asks people who they would like to be, more than 90% of them want to be someone else. If you spend your whole life trying to be someone else, then you are always going to be second best and not at all yourself.

Listen carefully: Until the day you die you are going to be you! Make peace with that. The Lord deemed it fit to make you, with your own unique personality, appearance and thoughts. He artistically designed you in your mother's womb, as David describes in Psalm 139. He planned your life in great detail long before you were born. You are the grand result of a divine design session.

Thank God for being you! Live your God-given potential to the full in unique ways every single day. Serve Him with your gifts, talents and personality like only you can. Only you can do that bit of work that the Lord created you for.

Day 48

Living Art

Let us then approach God's throne of grace with confidence, so that we may receive mercy and find grace to help us in our time of need.

– Hebrews 4:16 NIV –

David states in Psalm 139 that you are a unique creation of God. The Almighty God decided that you would specifically live in these times. God sketched your life on His easel. He planned you and called you into being. And then you were born. No, you are not a coincidence. God observes your life with great interest, every day. He notes everything that you do. He hears all your words. He reads all your thoughts.

God's expectation is that you will change in order to reflect His heavenly kindness, more and more. His desire is that you will let His light shine brightly in this dark world of ours. Not only did God form you with great care, and endless love, when Jesus carried your sins on His shoulders to the cross, He remodeled you into a new person. God interceded in your life once again through Christ, because He does not want you, one of His special works of art, to go to ruin.

Give thanks to God for having created you on His easel and for re-creating you. Start achieving your unique spiritual potential.

DAY 49

Dare

Do everything readily and cheerfully—no bickering, no second-guessing allowed! Go out into the world uncorrupted, a breath of fresh air. Provide people with a glimpse of good living and of the living God.
– Philippians 2:14-15 THE MESSAGE –

It is rather foolish to expect different results while you keep doing the same thing. Maybe you know these words. But do you believe them? Or are you a sheep? Repetition brings familiarity, and familiarity creates a feeling of security. Therefore, some people stay caught up in unhealthy situations for years. The fear of the unknown is a much greater threat to them than the fear of existing bad circumstances. It overrides the courage to explore new territory.

You will have to make a few very courageous choices if you don't want to remain a lifelong prisoner of yourself and your circumstances. You have to move forward in the name of the Lord if you want to discover new horizons. If you remain where you are now, you will never grow even one inch farther in the right direction. The Lord created you to be a lifelong explorer. There are thousands of treasures hidden in His Word and in His world for you to discover. Consider new things. Dare to make new choices. Go and live this challenge.

Day 50

Investor or Consumer?

"Do not store up for yourselves treasures on earth, where moths and vermin destroy, and where thieves break in and steal. But store up for yourselves treasures in heaven."

– Matthew 6:19-20 NIV –

There are two types of people: consumers and investors. Consumers use everything and everyone around them—people, friendship, money...No matter what you do for them, it is never enough. Somewhere in the future they are going to complain about the fact that you don't do enough for them. After all, they believe that you and life owes them!

Alternately, there is a small group of people who live from abundance, whom we'll call investors. They have enough, even though they have few material possessions. They are content. Investors have hope when the rest of the world is hopeless. After all, they live from the Lord's abundant treasure chambers of grace. How do you change from a consumer to an investor? Well, invest your life exclusively in God! Be content with Him. He is more than enough. God's heavenly treasure chambers overflow with grace, peace, freedom and love.

Become a daily partaker of His heavenly abundance. Then you will have more than enough. Then your cup will overflow!

Day 51

Faith Is...

Faith is confidence in what we hope for and assurance about what we do not see.

– Hebrews 11:1 NIV –

Faith is:

- the certainty that Christ did everything that I could not do myself, on my behalf, to make things right between me and God.
- to expect everything from God. Faith is not something that I have in me. My faith is never the issue, as if it is measurable. Faith just means that I place all my trust in Christ. He makes a new life possible!
- not a manner of changing life into a safe or predictable environment. Faith does not isolate me from surprises, shocks, disappointments, unexpected happiness or uncertainty. Ask Paul, who writes in 2 Corinthians 4 that he is also perplexed sometimes.
- a lifelong adventure. Faith asks the guts to follow Jesus in a courageous way, even if you do not know where the path is taking you because you lifted His cross onto your shoulders.

Faith is the certainty of Christ and His gift of salvation, even if you are not sure of what the next 24 hours holds in store. It is the courage to trust Him today, with your life and your eternal future.

Day 52

Gear Up for God

The LORD will vindicate me; Your love, LORD, endures forever.

– Psalm 138:8 NIV –

Your car doesn't move when it is in neutral. Neither does your faith. You have been recreated by God to do good things for Him in the ordinary moments of your life! You can't go to heaven if you remain stationary. In fact, Paul tells us in Ephesians 2:10 that God created you to devote your life to do those good deeds for which He prepared you. Are you turning this Scripture into truth?

Every moment of your life is precious. The next hour might just be a God-given opportunity in your life to do something profound in His name. During the mundane moments of your life, God sends opportunities your way.

However, no celestial warning lights are flashed. There aren't always angels who appear and shout, "Prepare yourself, God is going to start using you within 10 seconds." Instead, at the traffic light, at your desk or workplace, next to the sports field, or in class, these special moments arise out of the blue. Then you dare not act like an observer or a coward. No, then you must get into sixth gear for God.

Day 53

A Strong Fragrance

Thanks be to God, who always leads us as captives in Christ's triumphal procession and uses us to spread the aroma of the knowledge of Him everywhere.

– 2 Corinthians 2:14 NIV –

Faith smells. And it is a strong smell. In *The Message* Paul writes, "Everywhere we go, people breathe in the exquisite fragrance. Because of Christ, we give off a sweet scent rising to God, which is recognized by those on the path of salvation—an aroma redolent with life. But those on the way to destruction treat us more like the stench from a rotting corpse." We as Christians are Christ's aroma on earth. Some people think we smell badly. Others think that we have the scent of Life. What a contrast—life and death, salvation and destruction. All of this we exude if we live close to Jesus.

It is astounding that we are God's fragrance on earth. It is so sad that some people confuse the smell we have with that of death. They can't stand us because they are enemies of the cross of Christ. Nevertheless, it is our obligation to be Christ's aroma. We must distribute true life through our actions. How? Well, by living Christ's victory. But we must stay close to Him all the time. That is the secret. Then Christ's rejuvenating power flows through us to those who need it most.

Day 54

Radical

Trust in the LORD and do good.

– Psalm 37:3 NLT –

Sometimes spiritual opportunities arrive once only. Perhaps this is why the friends of the disabled man in Matthew 9 did something really radical. They decided to break down the roof of Peter's house, to lower their disabled friend down to Jesus. Talk about extreme!— tearing down a roof to get a sick friend to Jesus. Remarkable! The next day Jesus could possibly be gone and then the chance of a lifetime to bring their sick friend to Him would have disappeared.

Jesus couldn't ignore their pluck. All of a sudden they were in Jesus' personal space, in His face. That is radical faith. That is what happens when people only have one chance to change the world and to help others. Roofs have to be broken down. Appearance and etiquette are much less important than rejuvenating lives through Christ.

You have been nominated as an impact player in God's kingdom to make a difference today. Let your light shine. Leave your stamp on for all 24 hours that you have. Ensure that people who spend time with you in this time take note that you are a representative in Christ. Let your presence count!

Day 55
The Right Thing

If anyone, then, knows the good they ought to do and doesn't do it, it is sin for them.

– James 4:17 NIV –

Confucius once said, "To know what is right and not to do it, is the greatest deed of cowardice." James took it one step further by saying that he who knows how to do good and does not do it, sins, a contravention of God's will. James regards a life that is lived expressively as the best evidence of faith in God.

Faith cannot be merely expressed by a few confessions in church, or in discussions between people about what is right and wrong. Faith must become daily experiences. Faith in God must be spoken, done, seen, heard and felt. Otherwise faith is just words in the wind, cowardice or (even worse) sin! Did you hear that?

How much of what you know is right, is demonstrated every day, in your life? Perhaps I should not ask you this question, but rather your colleagues, family, friends, a shop assistant who helped you, or the guy at the grocery store. What will they say after having been in your company? Do they experience the love of God in your life? Well, why don't you ask them?

Day 56

Creating Opportunities

Let us not become weary in doing good, for at the proper time we will reap a harvest if we do not give up.

– Galatians 6:9 NIV –

Many people caution you to wait for the right moment. However, the problem is that many people wait for the right opportunities until the day they die. They spend their lives waiting in vain. For them, life is like a traffic light that never changes to green. I think it works the other way around, actually. God's way is always a green traffic light. You learn what His will is while you are on the move.

Of course there is space for standing still in our spiritual lives. But faith is not one long sequence of silence, passive moments in a celestial reception. Instead, it is about the right activities. Faith happens. And it happens in real life. It means seizing every spiritual opportunity, every day, like David who accepted Goliath's challenge as a wonderful opportunity to praise God. While the Israeli soldiers wondered how they could annihilate such a giant, David in turn wondered how he could miss such an enormous target with his five missiles! Do the same. Create opportunities to praise God, every day! Live abundantly, in praise of Him! Just do it!

Day 57
Radical Transformation

Guard your heart above all else, for it determines the course of your life.

– Proverbs 4:23 NLT –

Did you know that the dominant ideas in your head determine how you live? Your beliefs about other cultures, religions, your colleagues, church and family determine your entire life. Do you really know what your own stories sound like? Take some time to consider this for a moment. But also think about the following sentence that will change your life forever if you believe it: You have to radically invite the Spirit of God into your life to transform the main stories of your life!

It doesn't help if you give your heart to the Lord, but the ideas in your head remain your own. Millions of Christians have been caught in this trap. Their thoughts are controlled by stories other than those of the Lord. They still think selfish and loveless thoughts because they don't allow the Spirit to intervene. Far too few Christians live according to a brand-new story—the story of Jesus!

His story is always one in which humility, tenderness, sacrifice and faith triumphs. The story of Jesus is radically different from the dominant themes that feature in the lives of most people. What about you? Which story triumphs in you—those you have written yourself, or those of the Spirit?

DAY 58

Forget Un-Faith!

"Believe in the Lord Jesus, and you will be saved."
– Acts 16:31 NIV –

"I don't believe in God..." "God doesn't exist..." How often do we hear remarks such as these! It has become fashionable for people to confess their un-faith. Hollywood actors do it, sport stars do it, business people do it, even preachers do it. Un-faith is the in-thing! So, does this rise of un-faith mean that God is dethroned? A better question would be, was Christianity ever meant to be encapsulated in static institutions with strange rituals and professional clerics? Is this "official" face of Christianity the correct one? I don't think so.

The church is made up of people all across the globe who passionately follow Jesus. They frequently meet in church buildings, houses, offices...They are the church because they love Jesus as Lord. They are magnetic because they care for each other and for outsiders. Their love for Christ is translated into new deeds of kindness towards friends, strangers, outcasts, sinners and foreigners. They thrive amongst un-believers. Confessions of un-faith don't startle them. They know what they know. They believe what they believe, in spite of the efforts of evangelists of un-faith who feverishly want to convert others to their faithless views.

DAY 59

Use It or Lose It

Faith is confidence in what we hope for and assurance about what we do not see.

– Hebrews 11:1 NIV –

What were your resolutions for this year? Have you kept them after months have come and gone? It is quite possible that you haven't, because most people who make New Year's resolutions have forgotten them by the third week of January. However, it is not too late to begin over again. How about a new resolution to persevere on the road of God each day for the rest of the year? Remember, faith operates like the "use it, or lose it" rule in rugby. You cannot cling to last year's faith—consider it used up.

Faith is about keeping at it each day. Your faith must have an impact on your life here and now, otherwise it is archive material. If it does not have a daily impact, you belong in a museum for people of obsolete faith! Faith is entrusting Christ with your most precious possession—your life. Live your life each day in the knowledge that your faith is as alive as your most recent steps on God's road.

You must choose anew each day to follow the Lord with all of your heart. You need to decide daily to be obedient to Him in all things.

Day 60

The Robber of Faith

"That is why I tell you not to worry about everyday life—whether you have enough food and drink, or enough clothes to wear. Isn't life more than food, and your body more than clothing? Can all your worries add a single moment to your life?"
– Matthew 6:25, 27 NLT –

Do you know what one of the biggest stumbling blocks is that crosses the path of believers on a regular basis? Worry! It is a robber of faith. Worry kills our trust in God. In the parable of the sower (Matt. 13), Jesus tells us that the seed of the Word falls in four places. According to Him, 25% reject the gospel outright. But, a full 75% embrace the Good News. Can you believe it? Three out of every four people are very religious initially! Unfortunately, 50% of all those who hurriedly bow before God throw in the towel eventually. Why? Well, there are two reasons: a) the demands of religion, and b) worry! Those who hurriedly say yes to God all too soon backslide into the bad habit of worrying and running after money. Tragic, but true!

You have one of two choices—either you take God at His word when He promises to take care of you, or you try to do it yourself. If you carry out your daily tasks patiently, the Lord will provide for you at the right time.

DAY 61

The Heartbeat of Life

A nap here, a nap there, a day off here, a day off there, sit back, take it easy—do you know what comes next? Just this: You can look forward to a dirt-poor life, poverty your permanent houseguest!
– Proverbs 6:10-11 The Message –

Do you sleep through your own dreams every night, or do you experience them wide-eyed during the day? Do your dreams ever come true? Do you already live a small part of those plans God sowed in your heart as recently as yesterday? Or are you still stuck amongst the hopeless, waiting for better days to descend upon you from out of the blue? Are you actively present in every moment of your life, or are you still planning how you are going to report for a bit of playing time in real life? Well, then you are missing the true adventure.

Life happens one day at a time. God delivered it early this morning with heavenly compliments right to your doorstep. All you need to do is fill the day with all the right ingredients. Nobody else can do it on your behalf. You must choose to love the Lord, and to have an open heart and a merciful hand for others. You have to decide to live the right kind of life proactively.

Dare to do this! If you put this choice off until tomorrow, you are once again 24 hours too late.

DAY 62

Hope Floats

Guide me in Your truth and teach me, for You are God my Savior, and my hope is in You all day long.
— Psalm 25:5 NIV —

Good Friday is not really an appropriate name for the day Jesus died. It is definitely not good news when someone who came to adorn the world with so much grace had to pay for this by death. And yet the last words of Jesus on the cross give the right perspective to this Friday. Do you remember His words from to the Gospel of John, "It is finished"? Without a doubt! The price has been fully paid. The account is completely settled. The ledger between God and each person who embraces the redemption of Jesus has been balanced.

Hope floats. Hope does not sink into the sea of hopelessness; anger does not constantly win. Grace is the new password from heaven's gates. God and people can once again be good neighbors. Strangers and lost people may again sit down at God's table. Death definitely does not have the final say. Neither does all the injustice, hurt and suffering of the life in and around you. Because today there is an empty cross on Calvary!

Put your hand in the hand of the risen Christ and celebrate with Him at the festive table forever!

DAY 63

Treasures in Heaven

"Whoever becomes simple and elemental again, like this child, will rank high in God's kingdom."
– Matthew 18:4 THE MESSAGE –

Arnold Schwarzenegger, the famous Hollywood star and former governor of California once said something more amazing than some of the "famous" expressions he is known for, like "I'll be back," or the evergreen, "Hasta la vista, baby!"

He was trying to convince people that more money would not make them happier, "I now have $50 million, but I am just as happy as when I had $48 million." Absurd! But in an equally absurd world, where spending money on luxury items is more than four times higher, such statements should not surprise us.

How do we find that dividing line between "enough is enough" and "more" when we merely consider this in monetary terms? When will we learn from the book of Ecclesiastes (chapter 7) that those who regard money as everything will never have enough?

When will we start trusting in God as our heavenly Father who promises to give us everything that we need daily? Or are these nothing more than pious words from our side of the fence?

Day 64
On His Terms (Part 1)

You can make many plans, but the Lord's purpose will prevail.

– Proverbs 19:21 NLT –

It's not all about you! I am referring to your faith. God does not work for you. Not even your prayers are opportunities to give Him instructions concerning what He ought to do for you and others.

Really, consider this for a change, because many people walk around sulking about God. Apparently He did not help them when He was supposed to. He didn't take the illness away or He didn't stop the crime. Neither did He put food on the table quick enough. Consequently they walk around badmouthing God, saying that He is not kind or that He doesn't care anymore. Well, that happens because many of us have the idea in our heads that the Lord really owes us something. We serve Him, and therefore He has to do something for us in return!

Listen, the only reason why we serve God is because He is God. He mercifully redeemed us when we were lost. He loved us while we were still His enemies. He made us His own while we were so far away from Him. That is why we serve Him. It's all about Him. We serve Him on His terms.

Day 65

On His Terms (Part 2)

Let us run with endurance the race God has set before us.

– Hebrews 12:1 NLT –

God is not in our service; He does not work for us. We don't determine the conditions of the relationship. We should get to know God and serve Him as He reveals Himself to us in the Bible.

Fortunately, our God is a merciful God. He abounds in grace and abundantly shares it with each one of us. He pours out bucketfuls of kindness over us. His rest, His peace, His joy—that is what we receive if we walk with Him.

The Lord is our only strength when we are weak. He is our resting place when we are weary. He is our Hope when everything around us is hopeless. God is our shelter when we feel insecure. He is our only reason for living. He is our wealth and our rock.

The Lord is our oxygen, our breath, our entire lives. The Lord is with us in every storm. He walks with us through every dark valley and every straight road. He remains at our side until well past the finishing post.

Day 66

Taking Responsibility

"Where your treasure is, there your heart will be also."

– Matthew 6:21 NIV –

I hear you say you have no other choice but to live the hurried life you are currently living. There must be food on the table; the next house installment must be paid; groceries have to be bought; the kids' school fees are due…Yes, that may be true, but in the meantime you may be missing God's purpose for your life because you don't allow any quality time for Him in your life. Your life is a deadly race to get everything done.

With feeble excuses to justify your flustered lifestyle, you drive yourself even further towards burnout and hopelessness day after day. It looks like you still haven't noticed that your heavenly Father is looking after you. After all these years, do you still fail to realize that He knows exactly what you need (vv. 25-33)?

Start trusting in Him from now on to provide that which He knows you need. Take note, not what you think you need, but whatever He has decided! Find rest—the right kind of rest. Don't get stuck in the same old bad habits by living beyond your own speed limit.

DAY 67

Giving Time

Make the most of every chance you get. These are desperate times!

– Ephesians 5:16 THE MESSAGE –

If you are serious about your relationship with God, then give Him one of your most prized possessions today: your time! Most Christians don't think of this when they put things on the altar for the Lord. They offer their possessions, money, self-will, and a few other things, but not many give over their daily programs to the Lord!

To live a powerful Christian life, you have to give over your watch and your precious diary into the hands of the Lord. You have to learn to synchronize your time with the time of the Lord. If not, you will spend all of your time on the wrong things. Day-to-day faith is about surrendering your diary to the Lord each morning for Him to overwrite your priorities in heavenly ink with His heavenly ones. Your faith is truly at work when you repeat this giving-away exercise day after day and year after year.

Ephesians 5:16 (NIV) tells us that we should be "making the most of every opportunity, because the days are evil." Time is precious. Each day is there for you to walk with God, but if you let it slip through your fingers you waste a precious opportunity.

Day 68

True Life

Because of His great love for us, God, who is rich in mercy, made us alive with Christ.

– Ephesians 2:4-5 NIV –

It is not thanks to you that you are a Christian today. You were stone dead and covered in sin when God bestowed mercy on you the first time. Christ gave His life for you when you were still a sinner (Rom. 5:8). Even then He loved you. Why? Well, because God is love. He has a wealth of kindness (v. 4) and is a full-time grace farmer.

God loves the wrong people—sinners! He constantly tracks His enemies in order that He can save them. That is why He took you back as His child when you were farthest away from Him. God saved you when you did not want to be saved. He was the One who softened your hard-heartedness. He was the One who delivered you to life once again.

On top of that, Christ removed your heart of stone and replaced it with a heart that loves Him. You have received the greatest heavenly gift ever—a new life, with compliments of the living God. All of that just because you bow before Jesus as your Lord. Believe this good news whole-heartedly every day and live abundantly!

Day 69

Never Asleep

"Watch and pray so that you will not fall into temptation. The spirit is willing, but the flesh is weak."
– Matthew 26:41 NIV –

How quickly our strength wanes. Illness, worries and heavy schedules all too easily steal our life's fuel supply. Far too often we are tired, burnt out, dead beat. By the middle of the week, with the weekend hardly over, our flame burns low again. The good news is that God never becomes tired or sleepy. Psalm 121 tells us this good news. Age and illness have no effect on Him. He is never beset by boredom. Unlike we, who often doze off, God is always wide awake. When our knees buckle and our strength diminishes, God still remains strong.

More good news from Isaiah 44 is that not only is God strong when we are weak, but He renews the strength of His tired servants. He replenishes the strength of each and every one who perseveres in waiting for the Lord! That is His promise to you, too! Therefore, if you feel you are at the end of your tether, you need much more than vitamins or a weekend getaway—you need new strength that only God can provide. Knock on His heavenly door. Your portion of heavenly strength is right there waiting. Claim it in the name of Christ.

Day 70

Why So Safe?

"Walk with Me and work with Me—watch how I do it. Learn the unforced rhythms of grace."
– Matthew 11:29 The Message –

Orderly, structured, controlled—these words might describe your lifestyle. Do you live within a safe, highly structured routine where everyone and everything is in its right place? Wait, there is nothing wrong with a well-ordered life as such. But the question is: what do you do if an unexpected crisis descends upon you? Does the unexpected take you by complete surprise? Or is this an opportunity for growth?

Do you have the guts to see today as a clean, new page? Are you open and receptive to life's many surprises? Or is everything in your life so structured that you can even arrange your own "surprise party"? Do you still have the ability to see the Father's hand in a small act of kindness? Or in an unexpected smile, or a quick conversation?

Can you surprise yourself by changing your strict daily routine to visit somebody who is lonely, or to buy flowers for a loved one? Will you dare tell a colleague or a friend how God answered one of your prayers? Do you have the guts? Or do experiences like that disturb your set routines too much? Why so safe?

Day 71

Bold Prayer

So let us come boldly to the throne of our gracious God. There we will receive His mercy, and we will find grace to help us when we need it most.

– Hebrews 4:16 NLT –

John Maxwell once said that the most audacious prayer the average person prays every day is that evergreen prayer, "Lord, bless the food that we are about to eat!" Or, like many of us have adapted it, "Bless the hands that prepared the food." If that has become your main prayer, then you should also pray: "Lord, help me for I know not what I do!" Prayers are not formal recitations for the sake of tradition, or merely something I do to soothe my conscience. Prayer involves personally talking to the living God who holds heaven and earth in the palm of His hand.

Ecclesiastes 4 warns us to be careful with our words in the presence of the Lord. We have to count and consider our words very carefully because we are speaking to the King of the universe. We should know our place before Him. Every word that comes from our lips should be sincere. They must be chosen wisely! But it must also be bold—meaning that they should be encompassed in faith. We should trust God to uproot trees and plant them in the sea, as Jesus teaches us in Luke 17.

DAY 72

Powerful Prayer

"Ask, using My name, and you will receive, and you will have abundant joy."

– John 16:24 NLT –

Change all your prayers into regular sincere conversations with God. Choose a few Bible phrases to express your love for Him throughout the day, such as "Lord God, You are good" or "Praise the Lord." Continue doing this in times of crisis. Remind yourself in the words of the Bible that God will always be with you, and say it out loud to Him. "You shield me and keep me safe from harm because I walk close to You" or "The Lord is my Rock, my safe Haven."

Learn to use the Bible effectively by letting it become your guide in prayer also. Speak to God from His Word each day. Use the Psalms to help you share with God your own joy and sadness, your distress and pain. Be brief, sincere and to the point. Say what you have to, and say amen. Make prayer the heartbeat of your whole life before God. Continue to pray for everyone that crosses your path. Pray until heaven opens up in front of you.

Remember, the most important lesson of all is to always pray in the name of Jesus Christ.

DAY 73
A Prayer Away

"And when you pray, do not keep on babbling like pagans, for they think they will be heard because of their many words. Do not be like them, for your Father knows what you need before you ask Him."
– Matthew 6:7-8 NIV –

In his remarkable book, *Practicing the Presence of God*, written in the 17th century, Brother Lawrence says that in the course of the day you should pray several short, effective prayers, rather than one long, lifeless prayer aimed at merely easing your conscience. Jesus taught us in Matthew that God is not impressed by a shower of words. He is not interested in long prayers. That's not the point. Prayer never is an arm-wrestling session with God. In any event, we do not have anything with which to impress Him. God really needs nothing from us.

Prayer always requires faith, obedience and modesty. It always asks that we submit our will to His. Do you also want to pray effectively? Then change your prayers into honest, open discussions with God. Learn to use the Bible effectively as your most important prayer guide. Talk for shorter periods, but more often, with God, using the prayer guide, the Word.

DAY 74

The Speed of Prayer

"God, have mercy on me, a sinner."

– Luke 18:13 NIV –

Two of the shortest prayers in the New Testament are to be found in the Gospel of Luke. The one is in Luke 18:9-14 where the tax collector prays, "God, have mercy on me, a sinner." There and then, in a moment of heavenly grace, his prayer is answered. Jesus says that this man went home a changed person, someone whose relationship with God had been set right.

The speed of grace is always eons faster than the speed of light. It strikes you every time when you stand naked and bankrupt before God, with nothing else to offer Him than your sins and broken life. There is no speed limit to God's grace. He is always at His best when we are at our worst.

The second short prayer is in Luke 23:42 when the man on the cross next to Jesus asks, "Jesus, remember me when You come into Your kingdom." Jesus answers him, "I tell you the truth, today you will be with Me in paradise." There is no time to lose when people beg for mercy. God answers without fail and always at the speed of grace.

Day 75

Prayer

Rejoice always, pray continually, give thanks in all circumstances; for this is God's will for you in Christ Jesus.

– 1 Thessalonians 5:16-18 NIV –

Father of all grace and goodness,
In the name of Christ I rest at Your feet,
In still reverence I look up at You.
Your greatness is far too big for me to comprehend;
Your goodness is too overwhelming to understand,
But the little that I do grasp of You makes me joyful.
It causes me to leave myself and my loved ones
in Your care today.
Holy God, Your approval really counts the most of all;
Your love is all that matters.
That's why Your praise is all that's on my lips today.
And why my life wants to sing Your praise.
Teach me to serve You well.
Lord, please be merciful; Lord, be close.
Let Your light shine everywhere.
Let Your wisdom be our wisdom.
In Jesus' name,
Amen.

DAY 76
A Prayerful Life

Are any of you suffering hardships? You should pray. Are any of you happy? You should sing praises.
– James 5:13 NLT –

"We just need to pray more. Then God will bless our country," someone said. Everyone agreed. "How do you know that?" another person asked. "The Bible says so." "Yes," the rest agreed. "Where in the Bible do you read that prayer's primary function is to ensure safer circumstances for everyone?" this person continued. Again there was silence. Someone said, "It's written somewhere that you should 'pray and you shall receive.'"

"Yes, but does that mean that everything will suddenly be better if we send larger volumes of prayer up to heaven?" the questioner wanted to know. "Do you really think that there's a prayer meter that measures how long each of us prays and how many people pray for a particular matter and then these matters get a higher priority from God?"

He carried on, "Prayer is not a quick fix. It is primarily about God and His glory. If there is someone who needs to be changed by prayer, then it is primarily the one who prays himself." Then everyone started talking at the same time. Some agreed, some not. I walked away with some new perspectives on prayer.

Day 77

Light Years

The prayer of a righteous person is powerful and effective.

– James 5:16 NIV –

Here is a snippet of good news especially for you—the distance between heaven and earth is shorter than you've ever thought. On the day that the feet of Jesus touched the earth, this distance shrunk dramatically. On that day the chasm between heaven and earth was bridged forever. No longer do we have to rely on our own attempts to reach God. Such attempts will come to nothing in any case. Jesus Christ really is the only connecting road between God and us.

The best way to keep to Christ's road is through prayer. The minute you start praying you are present in the throne room of the Almighty. By way of a simple prayer in the name of Jesus you are transported to the presence of God in a divine instant. A prayer spans the distance between heaven and earth faster than any text message.

The speed of prayer easily beats any high-speed Internet connection. For a prayer to overtake the speed of light is plain sailing. Banish any distance between heaven and earth today in your prayers. Connect to God in the name of Christ.

DAY 78

How Far Away?

He tends His flock like a shepherd: He gathers the lambs in His arms and carries them close to His heart.

– Isaiah 40:11 NIV –

Are you one of those who wonder how far away God is? Maybe you feel that today He is very, very far. Well, the Bible tells you exactly how far away He is from you at this very moment. Listen, GOD IS ONLY A PRAYER AWAY! And no farther. He really is only a call-for-help away; no farther than a single humble prayer asking for help. He is as close to you as the time it takes you to speak one sentence in the name of His Son. Yes, God is as close to you as that.

Jesus removed the distance between God and you. Now, God is very near. You don't need binoculars or a telescope to see His goodness. And you don't have to shout at the top of your voice to get His attention. He is only one prayer away. That is all! When you address Him in the name of Christ, the last bit of distance is removed! Then you are as close to Him as a single prayer!

I repeat: When you pray in the name of Jesus, there is no distance between you and God. He is as close to you as that one prayer!

Day 79

Praying for Strangers

When God's people are in need, be ready to help them. Always be eager to practice hospitality. Bless those who persecute you. Don't curse them; pray that God will bless them.

– Romans 12:13-14 NLT –

Do you also sometimes get dispirited when you see yet another beggar standing at the side of the road? Or maybe someone trying to sell something? Next time, do something better than just ignoring them. Pray for them! Yes, you read correctly. Pray for them. Dare to place that unknown beggar before the Lord's throne. And who knows, maybe you will be the only person who would do such an "unthinkable" thing as praying for them.

While you are being so reckless praying for people who "accidentally" cross your path, why don't you also dare to pray to God on behalf of the expressionless person in the car next to you. Or for the shop attendant or the lady at the cash register. Instead of constantly glaring at your watch and wishing it was your turn to be served, you can fill the time with short prayers for unknown people, people with real names and real faces. Who knows what God can do with such quiet prayers!

Day 80

Submit to His Will

"Submit to God, and you will have peace; then things will go well for you."

– Job 22:21 NLT –

Prayer cannot be separated from the rest of your life. There is no such thing as rattling off a few quick prayers to still your conscience while carrying on as you wish. In John 15:7-8 Jesus tells us that if we remain in Him, we will receive what we pray for. A life of obedience to God is the road to, and the result of, a life of obedient prayer. Obedience to God changes the way you pray. Your prayers do not revolve around your own selfish needs then. They don't sound like someone shopping for groceries—"pass this, give me that, do this, help me here." No, then your prayers shift the attention away from yourself to the glory of God and the coming of His kingdom.

Believe me, prayer is a serious matter! Prayer is to speak with the King of the universe. Prayer can be a wondrous adventure if you pray in submission to God's will. If you do, the floodgates of heaven will be open above you night and day, because God hears and answers prayers such as these.

Go on, knock on the doors of heaven in the wondrous name of Jesus and see what happens!

Day 81

Forgiveness

Be kind and compassionate to one another, forgiving each other.

– Ephesians 4:32 NIV –

In one of his books, Ernest Hemingway tells the story of Paco who flees from his father after a disagreement and goes to live in Madrid. Later his father is so saddened by this that he posts an advertisement in the daily *El Liberal*: "Paco, all is forgiven. Meet me at Hotel Montana, noon Tuesday." That Tuesday, 800 boys named Paco showed up at the hotel.

It is easy to speak about forgiving…until you have someone to forgive, as C. S. Lewis says. It is easy to speak about forgiveness from pulpits. It is something completely different when you or your loved ones are the victims of injustice. Or when you are exploited by someone close to you. Well, here's a newsflash: you cannot forgive. You will never manage this yourself. But you know Someone who specializes in forgiveness. His name? Christ! Only He can, through His Spirit, help you to close those books and find new joy in life. Here's the route: take your darkest feelings to Him today. Put your hurt and unforgiveness on His shoulders. Also, leave it right there. Repeat this exercise every time that bitterness starts welling up in you.

Day 82

Good Deeds

"I'm telling the solemn truth: Whenever you did one of these things to someone overlooked or ignored, that was Me—you did it to Me."
– Matthew 25:40 The Message –

Life goes by all too quickly. Do not let the few years you have been granted slip through your fingers. Do you really gain anything by making a lot of money but losing the very people who are close to you? Above all, what do you gain if you are so busy that you don't have any time for God and you lose Him, too? Then you have literally lost everything!

Do the right thing here and now: go back to God immediately. He will receive you with open arms if you come before Him in the name of His Son. Also, go back to your loved ones—they will receive you as their honored guest.

Do something good for someone in the name of the Lord today. Do not go to bed without having spoken a kind word to someone or having performed a loving deed for someone in need. In Matthew 10:42, Jesus gives us the assurance that God will notice it if we give a cup of cold water to the most insignificant of His followers to drink. The smallest gesture of love is recorded in the most important place in the universe.

Day 83

Forgive and Forget

So what do we do? Keep on sinning so God can keep on forgiving? I should hope not!
– Romans 6:1 The Message –

In Matthew 18 Jesus teaches us that God does not work according to a quota system for forgiveness, like Peter thought. Initially, this disciple of Jesus thought that forgiveness granted seven times was more than enough. In those days the Jews believed that three times was sufficient, so Peter thought seven times was very generous. But then Jesus surprised His disciple with the heavenly formula—70 times seven. *Ad infinitum.* Endlessly. Constantly! God does not add up the times He has granted forgiveness. He does not keep record of the number of times you have asked His forgiveness. On the other hand, you don't have license to commit sin. Paul addresses this matter very clearly in this verse.

Grace does not give you a free pass to commit sin; on the contrary. But, if you commit sin, remember that you can be redeemed by God through Christ. Therefore, do not give up or allow yourself to be trapped in the mess you are in. At the same time, after you receive the phenomenal forgiveness of God, you should lavishly share it with others. Do not keep record of the times they have wronged you. Forgive and forget. Be finished with bitterness and reproach.

DAY 84

Memory Loss

The LORD is compassionate and merciful, slow to get angry and filled with unfailing love.
– Psalm 103:8 NLT –

Do you ever close that little black book in which you carefully record other people's mistakes and shortcomings? Do you go to bed angry night after night? Well, here's a newsflash if you struggle with amnesia regarding other people's misdemeanors: God suffers from memory loss. He gladly forgets people's sins, shortcomings, failures, wrong deeds, defects and factory faults. He doesn't worry about everything people do wrong against Him, as we learn in Psalm 103. Even better, He forgets every time, over and over again. For whom does He do this? Well, for everyone that knocks on His door in the name of Jesus.

God is forgetful when it comes to those things that people bring to Him in remorse. The reason? There's not enough storage space in God's heavenly home for all our written-off faults and paid-off accounts. The cross of Calvary is the permanent heavenly eraser in His hand. Grace says in five life-changing letters that God is on our side. It says that He fully loves us no matter how deep and far we have fallen. Grace says that God starts over time and again in our lives. He forgives and forgets. He closes old books forever.

DAY 85

I'm Shot

"The LORD your God is gracious and merciful."
– 2 Chronicles 30:9 NLT –

In the film *Black Hawk Down*, an officer looks at a vehicle filled with wounded soldiers. Then he spots a private named Othic and orders him to drive. Othic responds, "But, I'm shot, Colonel!" Then the colonel reacts with an amazing truth: "Everybody's shot! Drive!" What a metaphor for our own lives.

We all get wounded sometimes. Everybody's shot, actually! But we can still drive, because God is gracious and forgiving. He's not like us. When He forgives us we stay forgiven. God doesn't have the time or the energy to keep on reminding us of the wrongs of yesterday or the day before. No, He already pushed them out of the way because Jesus keeps on clearing our records.

The really great news is that God doesn't have a notorious little black book tucked away somewhere in heaven to remind Him of the nasty stuff we all did somewhere in our distant, or not too distant past. That black book was torn up ages ago when Jesus pleaded our case before Him successfully! In spite of our sins, God takes us in His service day after day. He loves us in spite of everything we do.

Day 86

Storage Space

Love does not demand its own way. It is not irritable, and it keeps no record of being wronged.
– 1 Corinthians 13:5 NLT –

Supermarkets normally require a vast amount of storage space for their stock. Perhaps you, too, require a lot of storage space in your house or apartment for food, clothes, furniture, PCs and books. Our mind is also full of stored information. If you are a Christian, then you definitely do not have storage space in your mind for bad thoughts about other people!

True faith is forgetful. It has the effect of never holding things against people. Time after time, in your head, you have to close the little black book which records other people's misdeeds. At the end of every day we must "delete" the negative information and transfer it to the dustbin for useless information.

In 1 Corinthians 13:5 Paul reminds us that God's people never keep a record of wrongs. Neither should you. You are a new person. "Remember to forget and forget to remember" when it comes to bad things. God has renewed your thoughts, which in any event do not have enough memory or bandwidth to store resentment or wrongs.

Day 87

Keeping Score

Make allowance for each other's faults, and forgive anyone who offends you. Remember, the Lord forgave you, so you must forgive others.

– Colossians 3:13 NLT –

Can you recall the question Peter put to Jesus in Matthew 18:21? "Lord, how many times shall I forgive my brother when he sins against me? Up to seven times?" Actually, Peter's offer was quite generous as the Jews thought forgiving someone three times was more than enough. That closed the books of forgiveness, and feelings of hate could multiply afterwards.

Jesus' reply was that seven times was not sufficient; 70 times seven would be in order. In other words, do not count the times you forgive your fellow man, for there is no end to forgiveness. Forgiveness does not work like sums of addition. The followers of Jesus do not keep record of others' mistakes, or of the times they have forgiven. They never think back on the transgressions of their friends, colleagues and family. Christians have a short-term memory when it comes to how others mess up. On the other hand, they are not blind to their own and others' flaws. However, they talk things over without being nasty about it. They never spread ugly rumors about others behind their backs. And they do not support hate speech.

Day 88

A Living Example

In everything set them an example by doing what is good. In your teaching show integrity, seriousness and soundness of speech that cannot be condemned.

– Titus 2:7-8 NIV –

Very early on in life children learn from grown-ups that only winners really matter. First place is the most important to many parents and teachers. The academic achievers, the first team, the executive committee of learners—they usually receive most of the attention. It is really wonderful if children can develop their talents and abilities from an early age. But does the pursuit of winning place the heartbeat of a happy life before God? Aren't grown-ups perhaps guilty of placing far too much pressure on children to be mini grown-ups?

Shouldn't children learn other crucial values in life other than just winning, winning, winning? Do they often enough see how we as parents serve the Lord with commitment? Do they see every day that we have open hearts and open hands for people less fortunate? Are we living examples of forgiveness and love towards others? Who then gives us the sole right to endlessly complain about the "youth of today" or to refer to them as the "lost generation"? Maybe we deserve this title! The young ones merely learn from us how to do it the wrong way!

Day 89

Your Greatest Critic

The LORD has done it this very day; let us rejoice today and be glad.

– Psalm 118:24 NIV –

We can be too critical of ourselves. Far too often we only focus on our faults and failures. Yesterday's errors remove all the joy from today's sunshine. Are you perhaps too hard on yourself? Do you find it difficult to forgive? In that case, adopt Lamentations 3:22-23 as your new daily creed. These are life-changing words, born out of the dark period directly after the Babylonian exile, when the Israelites returned to a devastated Jerusalem. Listen: The Lord's kindness never fails! If He had not been merciful, we would have been destroyed. The Lord can always be trusted to show mercy each morning.

Forget about yesterday's mistakes. Know that God's love is new, every day. Today He truly makes a fresh start with you and everybody else. Today is a new day in God's kingdom. The failures of yesterday and the day before are erased by the cross of Jesus Christ.

Notice today's new gift of heavenly mercy on your own doorstep. See God's footprints which obliterate your own. Then today's path is so much more accessible. You can make a success of every new day!

Day 90

Mistakes

Praise the Lord, my soul, and forget not all His benefits—who forgives all your sins and heals all your diseases.

– Psalm 103:2-3 NIV –

I am ashamed to admit that God often uses my mistakes for good, rather than my so-called obedience. It happened again just the other day. I lost my temper after receiving poor service in a shop. When I walked out of there, I felt bad about my sharp words to the shop assistant. I turned back submissively to apologize. The assistant immediately asked me why I had apologized. I shame-facedly mumbled that I was a Christian and that I had violated my life principles by speaking before considering my words. And all of a sudden this person wanted to know more about Christianity!

It is good to know that God not only works when I think He is working. It is just as nice knowing that the Lord does not really need me. It is through grace alone that He uses me with all my defects. Realizing that God loves me in spite of myself—well, that is earth-shattering good news!

Knowing that my sins never restrict His grace is also very liberating. But then I should not be content with Him using my mistakes alone. Then I am a very poor witness and a bad testimony for our wonderful Lord.

DAY 91

Grace and Forgiveness

Make a clean break with all cutting, backbiting, profane talk. Be gentle with one another, sensitive. Forgive one another as quickly and thoroughly as God in Christ forgave you.

– Ephesians 4:31-32 THE MESSAGE –

The guilty party in an illegal money-making scheme was caught and thrown into jail. Everyone in the local community, where this fraudster was also a well-respected leading figure, was deeply shocked. Many of them lost their life savings. Shortly afterward, the local priest preached a sermon where he praised God that justice was done and that this man was behind bars. He seriously prayed that the church members would be repaid their losses.

When a congregation member who also lost everything suggested that they all visit the fraudster in jail and pray for him, everyone was shocked. "We are not ready for that. Our people got hurt too badly," was the official reply. The man decided to go alone. In jail, he knelt next to the fraudster who had robbed him. Together they prayed for grace and forgiveness. That day the Lord's grace was visible in the jail. Christ showed up there as Savior. Thereafter, these two started a wonderful prison ministry. And the religious townspeople? Well, they remained bitter.

Day 92

The Vine

"I am the vine; you are the branches. Those who remain in Me, and I in them, will produce much fruit. For apart from Me you can do nothing."
– John 15:5 NLT –

The scene, Luke 13:6-9: The parable of the fig tree that did not bear fruit. The main characters: God (the Owner), Jesus (the Gardener), and me (the tree without fruit).

The solution to not bearing any fruit: A season of grace! Jesus undertakes to fill my life, inside and out, with heavenly water and fertilizer. He does not simply grant me a year's grace to see what I will do with it. That would not be true grace, because it would still leave the ball in my court. Divine grace does not work that way. No, Jesus gives me a chance now! He takes sole responsibility for seeing to it that I bear fruit. Jesus puts His name in jeopardy. He takes the chance Himself.

Do I have to do anything? Yes, I only have to be in the vineyard! That is all. Christ looks after the rest. He does the watering and the fertilizing. I simply have to be there in the season of grace when He works on my life.

Where is the vineyard? The vineyard is where the Word is. The vineyard is when I pray. The vineyard is where believers get together and spread the gospel. Be there.

DAY 93

Start with Today

"Give us today our daily bread."

– Matthew 6:11 NIV –

Many people live in the future already. But they show up here in the present every day. In fact, they merely regard today as a fleeting moment on the road to tomorrow. Here and now is not really important. For them the meaning of life lies in tomorrow. That is a big mistake. Jesus taught us to live today, to live from here towards the future, not the other way around. In the Lord's Prayer we are taught to pray, "Give us today our daily bread," not tomorrow's bread.

In Matthew 6 we are taught not to worry today, about tomorrow's problems. Life happens today. God's grace is here today. His care, love and support as well. Tomorrow is at least a day away. A lot of water has to run into the ocean before today becomes tomorrow.

What a waste of time it is if today we don't fully live to the glory of God. What a waste to think that we are only going to get around to living to His glory tomorrow or next week. No, today is the day. Go, and receive your portion of grace from God. Give your life to Him today. Then you are living correctly!

Day 94

Awe

Put yourself aside, and help others get ahead. Don't be obsessed with getting your own advantage. Forget yourselves long enough to lend a helping hand.
– Philippians 2:3-4 The Message –

The world is becoming cynical. Nobody believes anything good about anybody else anymore. When somebody is successful, she or he is maligned. When somebody wins, others "steal" his or her medal by making sarcastic comments behind his or her back. Nobody is safe from the cynical comments of other people. Should we not trade in our cynical hearts for hearts full of wonder? How? Well, start by doing what Paul said in Philippians 2. Start by treating others as more important than yourself. Notice that God gives His grace in large quantities to the people at work and in the church. Remember, you are not the only person whose prayers are heard. See the beauty in friends and family despite the scars that life has inflicted on them. For a change, look past their faults; look until you see how God also blesses them with His grace.

Awe makes you smaller and others bigger. As you become smaller before God, so your cynical nature disappears. The more Christ's heartbeat echoes within you, the more you discover the beauty in others.

Day 95

God Likes Me

"We believe that we are all saved the same way, by the undeserved grace of the Lord Jesus."

– Acts 15:11 NLT –

God does not owe us anything. He is not in our service. What can we do for Him so that He owes us anything in return? In Romans 11, Paul says that God does not like us as a result of who we are. No, He loves us despite who we are. This is called grace, the type Paul refers to in Romans 5:

At just the right time, when we were still powerless, Christ died for the ungodly (v. 6).

God demonstrates His own love for us in this: While we were still sinners, Christ died for us (v. 8).

If, when we were God's enemies, we were reconciled to Him through the death of His Son, how much more, having been reconciled, shall we be saved through His life (v. 10).

Powerless, sinners, enemies—that is who we were when God encountered us, by no means strong, victorious or nice! He loved us when we were knee-deep in muck. Despite ourselves—that is how God likes us most! His love says so much more about Him than about us. That is what He is like. He does not owe us anything, and yet He dispenses grace to us every day.

Day 96

Hijacked by Grace

"Prove by the way you live that you have repented of your sins and turned to God."

– Matthew 3:8 NLT –

The young Paul was like a man possessed when he heard the followers of Jesus claim that He was the resurrected Messiah. No one who died on a cross could be the Messiah. It was blasphemy! Paul persecuted the followers of Jesus with a vengeance everywhere he went.

Then, one day, he encountered Jesus on the road to Damascus. This meeting altered his entire life. A true revolutionary was born that day when Jesus and Paul met face-to-face, one that redefined religion and life for millions of people throughout history. Talk about impact!

After being "hijacked by grace", Paul's new purpose took him on dangerous, yet adventurous journeys to the farthermost corners of the world. He travelled more than 11,000 miles on foot during his various missionary journeys across the Roman Empire. The new Paul who instantly turned into a loyal follower of Jesus had a new vision, one that provoked, disrupted and challenged everyone and everything around him, but one that made a huge impact, the right kind! Perhaps we should follow suit.

Day 97

Darkness or Light?

You are a chosen people, a royal priesthood, a holy nation, God's special possession, that you may declare the praises of Him who called you out of darkness into His wonderful light.

– 1 Peter 2:9 NIV –

Somebody said to me that the future looks rather bleak. "What future are you talking about?" I asked. "Do you mean the future in three months' time? Or the one in five years' time? We are now living the future we were so worried about five years ago!" And yet those of us who are living get by! Amazing! No, it is sheer grace! It is all thanks to God! He is really faithful! God has ensured that we made it to today! And, furthermore, He has brought the bread of mercy right to our doorstep.

Are you without bread today? No? Do you have enough blankets on your bed? Yes? Will you have enough bread to eat for the next month? Definitely! Will your health make it through today and maybe even tomorrow? Indeed! Then why are you so worried? Why do you complain that there is no future? This constitutes a motion of no confidence in your heavenly Father. He guarantees that He will give you bread for today. He, who takes care of the birds and the flowers, will care for you. His grace will be enough for you every day, yes, more than enough!

DAY 98

Divine Grace

Be kind and compassionate to one another, forgiving each other, just as in Christ God forgave you.
– Ephesians 4:32 NIV –

The gracious heart of Jesus beats warmly for the losers of His day. Those who got a red card from the religious leaders were at the top of His gracious list.

Think about the prostitute in Luke 7. She wiped her tears from the feet of Jesus using her hair, after she burst in uninvited on a dinner where Jesus was the Guest of Honor. While the pious choked with indignation over the fact that Jesus forgave her sins, she heard the most beautiful words ever: "Your faith has saved you; go in peace." No wonder the religious leaders later had Him killed. They couldn't stand the fact that Jesus gave away God's kindness for free to people like her.

The grace Jesus offers isn't even cheap; it is completely free! But that is exactly what Jesus is like, even today! You are always welcome in His company, no matter how deep or far you have fallen. With Him there is always an extra portion of heavenly grace to be had! All you need to do is ask.

Day 99

Into the Storm

Grace and peace to you from God our Father and the Lord Jesus Christ.

– 1 Corinthians 1:3 NIV –

When George Bush and Tony Blair, the two most influential leaders in the world at one stage, were hot on the heels of Saddam Hussein, he was hiding in a sewer pipe in Bagdad.

When the pope and the emperor declared him to be enemy number one, Martin Luther translated the New Testament into German. That is what the heroes of the Lord do; they walk even deeper into the storm. The more fierce the battle, the more firmly they stand at their posts.

Martin Luther single-handedly faced the wandering church of his day and then chose the way of God. Contrary to everyone else, He submitted to the graceful words of the Bible. His love for God overruled his fear of people. That is why Luther nailed his 95 statements to the church door in Wittenberg, Germany, in 1517, which finally catapulted the church in a new direction.

Henceforth, grace was once again present in the church. Divine grace once again sparkled like the sun. Are you also living with God's grace? Is your faith built on Christ alone? And is the Word your only guide?

DAY 100

Unconditional Love

What marvelous love the Father has extended to us! Just look at it—we're called children of God!
– 1 John 3:1 THE MESSAGE –

I'm sold out on Philip Yancey's definition of grace. In his book *What's So Amazing about Grace?* he says there is nothing we can do to make God love us less, and there is nothing we can do to make God love us more. He loves us regardless. God loves us on Christ's behalf. He loves us despite ourselves, not because of who and what we are. God's amazing love is not performance driven; it is always relationship based. Listen again...He doesn't look at who does the most for Him and then loves those people more. He doesn't love us more when we are obedient and less when we fail.

God is our Father. That's why His love for us is a constant reality. It comes without a performance clause that's flourishing everywhere in the business world. Grace is nothing more different than God's free caring for us. Grace is a godly verb. It says that Jesus is on our heels with a handful of fresh goodness. That's why grace is also a rest-word for you and me. Now then, stop running. Go and rest in God's arms. He'll do the rest. He loves you.

Day 101

Pay It Forward

"I have been a constant example of how you can help those in need by working hard. You should remember the words of the Lord Jesus: 'it is more blessed to give than to receive'"

– Acts 20:35 NLT –

Try to give away something of yourself: a few precious seconds, some coins, a gift, a set of clothes, a visit to someone who is lonely, a prayer, a gentle hand on someone's shoulder, a listening ear. Paul tells us that Jesus said it makes us happier to give than to receive. Believe it; do it! One of the pillars of the gospel is to give. Jesus is the perfect example of this. He gave everything. His own life was His gift to all of us.

To give brings your life in sync with the gospel. Then you live according to the basic tenets of God's kingdom. In this world everybody wants to receive as much as possible. In God's world, His people give a part of themselves. The more they give without expecting to receive something in return, the more heavenly joy streams into their world. And their dungeons become shallower.

Eventually they are only as deep as a shallow fish pond, and on a good day the dungeon disappears completely! To give genuinely is to have something of God's character. It results in experiencing abundance with God.

Day 102

The Winning Team

With God we will gain the victory, and He will trample down our enemies.

– Psalm 108:13 NIV –

To follow Jesus is to be on the winning side of the battle. It is to be in the presence of the One who hands out abundant life, here, now and forever. However, to be a disciple of Jesus is definitely not a walk in the park. It's no easy route.

To be a disciple of the Messiah is to live against the grain. It is to live dangerously in the storms. It is to be a living example of God's brand-new day in the kingdom. It is to know that His shalom is a present reality in His Son, Jesus. Actually, this is the battle cry and victory song of His followers!

Jesus is the only one strong enough to fight Satan. He already conquered the forces of darkness at Calvary. Jesus rose from the dead. He sits at the right hand of God. He has all power in heaven and on earth. Through faith in Him the Evil One is cast out! To live for God is to fight the battle the right way.

To live victoriously and beautifully for Jesus is to show no sympathy for the devil.

DAY 103

A Hungry World

Be an example to all believers in what you say, in the way you live, in your love, your faith, and your purity.

– 1 Timothy 4:12 NLT –

"If you are not a good example, at least be a horrible warning!" Nowadays there are various adaptations of these words, "Don't do as I do, do as I say!" Ouch! How can I dare expect something from somebody else when I am not prepared to do it myself? That would not be right, because it would mean that I am deceitful, a warning of how others should not live.

If I am a follower of Jesus, He calls me every day to live and practice His kind of life filled with love and servitude. I need to model it in all I say and do. I never have the luxury of doing as I please or hiding behind my flaws and weaknesses.

No, I answer to a Lord whose burden is light. And to a Lord who isn't always ready and waiting to judge me.

DAY 104

Reflecting God

Live a life filled with love, following the example of Christ. He loved us and offered Himself as a sacrifice for us, a pleasing aroma to God.

– Ephesians 5:2 NLT –

Martin Luther King, Jr. once said that even if you have a lowly job you should do it with the same commitment and enthusiasm that Michelangelo relied on when he was sculpting his great works, or that Mozart used in composing his genial music. That's also what Paul meant when he wrote in Colossians 3 that everything we do and say should glorify God. Put another way, the Lord's name should preside in CAPITAL LETTERS over every word we speak and everything we do. Like a flashing advertising board, our lives should reflect God's splendor and importance.

How do you live your life in the right CAPITAL LETTERS? Well, you invite God humbly to be the Guest of Honor in your life every day. Ensure that He's the Guest of Honor in every conversation you have. Then all your words will be carefully chosen, tasteful and uplifting. Ensure that the Lord is the Witness to everything you do. Then your work will be done for His glory alone and not primarily for your boss or company. Then you'll do your work with pride, thoroughness, and commitment. Your light will shine for Christ in new ways.

Day 105

Unfashionable

We are being transformed into His image with ever-increasing glory, which comes from the Lord, who is the Spirit.

– 2 Corinthians 3:18 NIV –

"You have to take me just as I am," a difficult church member told me once. "Why?" I asked. "Well, that's just how it is since I'm not going to change," he replied. "No, you're wrong," I said. Second Corinthians 3:18 teaches us that God's Spirit transforms us into the likeness of Christ with ever-increasing glory. We are definitely not lifelong victims of ourselves, our education or circumstances. We don't have the luxury of staying as we are for the rest of our lives. Christ gives us the grace and the privilege to change and grow.

Too many people around us are victims of this "I can't change" syndrome. That's why negative issues such as our deep-rooted prejudices toward each other still run strong, despite our "deep religiosity." Does this happen because we believe we have the right to think like we always did? Or maybe because we ourselves are such bad examples of true transformation in this area? Listen, we can change. No. Father God can change us…and He will!

DAY 106

Be the Difference

Keep your eyes open, hold tight to your convictions, give it all you've got, be resolute, and love without stopping.

– 1 Corinthians 16:13-14 THE MESSAGE –

Is it only my imagination or is selfishness presently the order of the day? Not to mention hate, suspicion, and fear. Have the headlines of the world now become the headlines of Christians as well? Are we following the example of the Pharisees only to do good to those who will return the favor, and to hate our enemies? Do we follow Jesus just as long as it is comfortable? Let's break this vicious circle. Let's follow the advice of Romans 12 by showing kindness to our opponents. Let's make those that stand against us red with shame by repaying their anger with goodness. Let's pray that the Lord will teach us what it means to follow Him. Let's remember that God's route is not only the road to church on Sundays. Let's allow the Holy Spirit to free us from hate and suspicion.

We can bring joy to at least one other person today through a text message, a call, or a quick visit. Then our own life-cup will be filled automatically. We can allow Jesus to let His love flow through us like a stream of living water (John 7:38). We can break this stronghold of selfishness in the name of Jesus.

DAY 107

Bearing the Cross

"Whoever wants to be My disciple must deny themselves and take up their cross and follow Me."
– Matthew 16:24 NIV –

Gordon Wakefield writes that there can never be a hint of true Christianity without a cross—the cross of Christ that we bear, and each of us bearing our own cross. From the manger to the cross, from Bethlehem to Calvary, and from there all the way to my own life—that's the nutshell story of faith. From the cross of Jesus to the cross that I have to carry on His behalf—that's the new route that I follow.

When I become part of Jesus' story, it turns me into someone who is crucified and cross-bearing in the same instant. The story of Jesus says loud and clear that my life started over from square one.

At the manger, the cross and the empty grave I find my new identity. From there I also find the daily direction for my life. Jesus is my only compass. His arrival, His death and His resurrection are the reasons for my existence. That's why I can tap my own little drum for Him today, even while there's a heavy cross resting on my narrow shoulders. That's why I can follow Him all the way, because He sacrificed all for me as well.

DAY 108

Past and Present

Create in me a pure heart, O God, and renew a steadfast spirit within me.

– Psalm 51:10 NIV –

Once, I thought I had to impress other people. No longer. As a follower of Jesus, I don't want to impress, I only want to share impressive God-stories.

Once, I thought I had all the answers. No longer. As a follower of Jesus, I have more questions than answers.

Once, I had everything under control, or thought I did. No longer. As a follower of Jesus, I surrender all control to God who is in charge of everything.

Once, I enjoyed receiving more than giving. No longer. Now, as a follower of Jesus, I experience the joy of giving and sharing with people around me.

Once, nothing impressed me much. No longer. Now as a follower of Christ, I see beauty everywhere.

Once, I talked mostly about God. No longer. As a follower of Jesus, I talk more to God.

Once, I was excited about complex theological ideas. No longer. As a follower of Jesus, I am more excited about interacting with people who follow in His footsteps.

Once, people had to listen to me most of the time. No longer. As a follower of Jesus, I take more time to listen to others.

Day 109

Reflecting His Love

Imitate God, therefore, in everything you do, because you are His dear children. Live a life filled with love, following the example of Christ.
– Ephesians 5:1-2 NLT –

Do you remember the earliest term used to refer to the first Christians? If you say "believers," you are not quite right. They were called "People of the Way" (Acts 9:2). The first believers were not known for what they knew, but for the way in which their lives were a testimony of their faith in Jesus. They did not have a confession of faith, but lived a life that confessed their faith. In all the right ways, their lives spoke louder than their words.

The testimony of the first Christians was a daily testimony. Others saw how they loved the Lord and one another and how they supported people in need. Their testimony was founded in a magnetic lifestyle of prayer, compassion and simplicity. That is why they were known as People of the Way—the Way of Jesus. Their faith was clearly visible in their new relationships. What a pity that today we are known more for confessions of faith on paper than for our lives filled with love for God and others. How sad that the main conversations of churches often revolve around "purity of doctrine" and not about "purity of life." Are we missing something or Someone?

Day 110

Tapping the Drum

"This will be a sign to you: You will find a baby wrapped in cloths and lying in a manger."

– Luke 2:12 NIV –

Do you know the "pa rum pump um pum" refrain from *The Little Drummer Boy*? This song tells the story of a boy who wants to play the drums with all his might for the child in the manger.

The arrival of Jesus calls for festivity. That's what the three wise men realized when they saw His star. Their gold, incense, and myrrh herald of the arrival of the Child of Peace here on earth.

But the coming of Jesus is about so much more than just presents. It's about us becoming living presents to others. Just as Jesus came to give Himself away without any preconditions, He turns us into gifts to those around us.

But there's more about the coming of Jesus that we need to know…if we only stand in awe at His manger, we haven't yet walked far enough. We also need to bow down at the cross of our Messiah. The manger calls for the cross. The gifts of the wise men call for the gift of Jesus to us all. His own life is the real gift. His precious life is God's ultimate gift to the whole world.

Jesus is new life for us all. That's why we celebrate His coming the whole year round.

DAY 111

One Step at a Time

God's way is perfect. All the LORD's promises prove true. He is a shield for all who look to Him for protection.

– Psalm 18:30 NLT –

I admire people whose lives are so neatly organized. And those who pray and quickly receive an answer. But I have to add that I am astonished at the number of church members who think that prayer is an easy shortcut, an instant quick fix. On my side of the fence it is not that easy.

I associate myself with John Eldredge, who writes in his best-seller *Waking the Dead* that he experiences approximately 20 bright days per year when he knows exactly what God expects of him. The rest of the time God's will seems to him like driving in dense fog. Maybe you know that feeling, too. Well, then you will appreciate the words of Oswald Chambers, the missionary giant who touched so many lives: "I never see my way. I never have far-reaching plans."

Maybe God does not specialize in five- and ten-year plans. He mostly does things one day at a time, like Exodus 16 and the Lord's Prayer teaches us. Let us find His way for today, then at least we can live on course one day at a time!

Day 112

Hard Work

Always give yourselves fully to the work of the Lord, because you know that your labor in the Lord is not in vain.

– 1 Corinthians 15:58 NIV –

Some people like to complain about how hard they work. Then I say something to the effect that the license on hard work has already been snatched up by someone else. Or that hard work is not an Olympic sport that qualifies for medals. I wonder whether some people think that hard work is somehow an achievement that earns them bonus points. Or something that others should admire you for.

I constantly remind myself of the story Jesus told in Luke 17:7-10 where He says if I have done everything for the Lord that I should have, then I don't deserve a standing ovation from Him or others. Hard work in His vineyard is a normal part of my calling. In the end, I am merely God's servant. Everything I do for God I should do diligently, without expecting any recognition. It is my life's commission to do God's will.

Hard work very often goes hand in hand with a life devoted to God. No, it is never about merit, as if the Lord should reward me if I do my share. On the contrary, it is all about gratitude for the opportunity of being able to work for Him.

DAY 113

Pious Words

Show me Your ways, LORD, teach me Your paths.
– Psalm 25:4-5 NIV –

Recently I watched a reality show about women competing for the hearts of a number of men. One lady, who wasn't chosen, said afterwards that everything happens for a reason. If Jesus wanted this guy to pick her, then He would ensure that it happened. Conversely, the woman who was chosen said that she had simply trusted in the Lord and that her dream had come true. It sounded to me like these women regarded themselves as passive victims of God's will. Had they perhaps forgotten that they had willingly entered into this show and actively taken part in it?

Paul says in 1 Corinthians 4 that we are joint managers of God's earthly household. Consequently we have to take joint responsibility for our choices. Maybe we too easily hide behind clichés like "there is a purpose to everything." Rash pronouncements about the will of God are dangerous. He is the Lord and we are only ordinary people.

We should have more respect and reverence for Him. We have to learn to count our words carefully in His presence. Perhaps we should try to be more humble when we talk about God's will.

Day 114
Spiritual Traffic Jams

The Lord has told you what is good, and this is what He requires of you: to do what is right, to love mercy, and to walk humbly with your God.
– Micah 6:8 NLT –

Nowadays you can hardly travel on a freeway without getting caught in a traffic jam, not to mention peak time, when you sit stuck behind hordes of cars. Some church members are also caught up in spiritual traffic jams. They spend their whole lives sitting at an imaginary red traffic light, waiting for the spiritual light to turn green so that they can get going for God.

Some think you have to wait for months and years for God to make His plans known to you. Until then, they sit around passively in spiritual traffic that isn't making any progress in the right direction. Such people simply talk of their intention to one day do something big for God. But they never get around to actually doing it!

Listen, God's will is a road with a green traffic light. You discover His plans while you are driving. You find God's will while you are living the right life for Him. It really doesn't help much if you are constantly stationary on the right road. Get going. Experience and do God's will today.

Day 115

Opinions

Your words are my joy and my heart's delight.
– Jeremiah 15:16 NLT –

"Everyone is entitled to an opinion," someone says. "And to their own idea of the truth," he adds. "Yes, surely, but does that mean that all opinions are equal?" I wanted to know. Danger lights start flashing when every thinkable opinion is considered to be valid. Of course we can look at life in many different ways, but there is also right and wrong. This applies from traffic rules to the most basic questions about God and life.

My compass for truth is the Bible. It is the life book for everyone who wants to live in tune with God's will. No, the Bible is not a book to hurt others with. Nor is it a verse book from which a few favorite texts can be drawn arbitrarily and the rest forgotten. It is also not a scientific handbook by which today's scientists need to be proven right or wrong.

When the Bible is read correctly, it becomes medicine. The Bible is a compass pointing directly to Christ. But then I need to read it book by book and understand the context within which it was written correctly. Then the Bible shapes my conscience correctly and in the right direction.

DAY 116

The Harbor or the Storm?

I know the LORD is always with me. I will not be shaken, for He is right beside me.

– Psalm 16:8 NLT –

Think about the following question: Where do you discern God's will the clearest—in the harbor, or in the storm? Let me explain—with the harbor I mean the well-known religious terrain among fellow believers in church or Bible studies. The storm represents the everyday world with its unpredictability, dangers, unbelievers, and challenges. Listen to that question again: Where do you discern God's will the clearest—in the harbor or in the storm?

Let me make it easier. Think about Jesus' behavior on earth. Now, where did He spend most of His time—in religious harbors, or in dangerous storms? Was Jesus more often among the religious, or more often among the doubters, sinners, outcast, strangers, losers…? I think you know the answer—obviously Jesus spent more time amongst the non-religious! Why? Because He came specifically for those people, as He says in Mark 1.

If it's true that Jesus spent more time in the storms than in the "safe harbors," where should we then spend most of our time? In the storm, of course. Now why are we always trying to discern God's will in spiritual harbors? Let's all get back to stormy waters.

DAY 117

Charging into the Storm

Whether you turn to the right or to the left, your ears will hear a voice behind you, saying, "This is the way; walk in it."

– Isaiah 30:21 NIV –

Some people are wandering around aimlessly in the wind and the weather. We should be there for them. We should serve and love them in the name of Jesus, without writing them off. Why do we then spend more time sitting in religious harbors than serving and helping out there on the open sea? Is God's will not clearly audible, visible, and tangible when we are among the poor, the lonely and the lost? Who knows, maybe that's the reason why so many believers never find God's one and only will for their lives...they're not at the right place often enough—out there in the storm where Jesus is busy saving people who drown in their own sins and shame!

How do you get into God's rhythm of navigating the storms of life? Well, there are no quick recipes or shortcuts. It's a lifelong journey of humility, obedience, reflection on God's will, and carefully listening for the voice of His Spirit. He'll teach you how to survive and thrive in the storm. He'll help you over and over again how to be the hands and feet of Christ and how to touch the lives of those in serious need of grace.

Day 118

In Step with God

He is your example, and you must follow in His steps.

– 1 Peter 2:21 NLT –

The right question is not "What is God's will for my life?" but "What is God's will?" and how do I obey it? Did you notice the shift in emphasis? God's will is not about me. No, it is about God, 24 hours a day, seven days a week, 365 days a year. It's about His honor, His plans, His dreams, His will!

The only way my plans can synchronize with those of God is when I walk in step with Him. When my diary is replaced by the diary of the living God, and my watch is traded in for a heavenly hourglass, the right things start happening in my life. That is when God's will is done.

How does this happen on ground level in my life? Well, it all starts with prayer. Jesus taught us to pray, "Let Thy will be done!" God's will in your life is not done automatically, but you can miss out on it by being disobedient. The way to get back on track is by praying in faith, praying those getting-in-step-with-God prayers! Your life should be like clay in the hands of God every day—good quality clay that is soft and malleable.

Day 119

Perfect Timing

For God says, "At just the right time, I heard you. On the day of salvation, I helped you." Indeed, the "right time" is now. Today is the day of salvation.
– 2 Corinthians 6:2 NLT –

God does two great things every day: He provides heavenly bread to all His loved ones (Exod. 16) and He also hands out brand-new life (2 Cor. 4).

God is on duty today. In fact, He reports on time for every day. Throughout the ages God has always appeared to help and assist everyone who calls Him by name. God is the God of today. God has many glorious yesterdays behind Him, and tomorrow there will be an enormous victory procession when Christ returns. But today is His day, now; it is His day for work, His day for caring, His day for sharing His mercy.

Today is the day of salvation, as Paul writes in Corinthians. He cannot wait for tomorrow as it is too far into the future. Today God wants to share His bread with you and give away abundant life. Today He wants to change the world. Today He wants to adorn your life with His heavenly grace. Are you on time for His great plans? Or are you still lingering around, lost in yesterday?

Day 120

Spiritual Finesse

Start with God—the first step in learning is bowing down to God; only fools thumb their noses at such wisdom and learning.

– Proverbs 1:7 The Message –

Some people have it, others don't. I'm speaking about spiritual finesse. In the book of Proverbs it's called wisdom. Wisdom, the type that starts with reverence for God according to Proverbs 1:7, touches your daily life dramatically. This kind of wisdom is to know when to say your say, and when to keep your mouth closed. It's to never storm blindly into any situation with an artificial quick fix. Wisdom makes you dare to do God's will, but also be mindful of the traps of folly.

Spiritual finesse is to know the difference between wisdom and folly and to apply that knowledge wisely. Where do you find this type of finesse? Listen afresh to Proverbs where it's taught that it all starts with a life of dedication to God. Wisdom is equal to full-time, day in and night out respect for the Lord. This type of wisdom is the reason why you can't help but treat other people with respect. Respect for God continually flows over into respect for other people.

Such a life filled to the brim with spiritual finesse causes you to read the "handle with care!" sticker on others every time…and to respect it!

Day 121

From the Inside Out

"People judge by outward appearance, but the LORD looks at the heart."

– 1 Samuel 16:7 NLT –

We spend most of our time getting our lives sorted out externally. Consider our domestic routines: our clothes are neatly packed in cupboards, food is stored in pantries and our cars are parked in garages. The greatest part of our time, money and energy is taken up with tangible things like clothes, cars, houses, the acquisition of possessions and our appearance.

Paul writes in 1 Corinthians 3:16 that we who believe in Christ are a temple of the Holy Spirit. We are God's new home here on earth. God does not reside in church buildings. We are His house, His spiritual temple. And yet many of our spiritual houses are derelict, because we spend too much time on our external dwellings. We believe the lie that life actually happens externally.

God teaches us that we do in fact operate differently. There is only one way to live our lives from the inside out: we must give the Holy Spirit free access to our lives, from the inside out. We must be soft clay in the Sculptor's hands so that He can decorate us with His love and mercy. Then we will live the way God wants us to.

Day 122

Set Your Sails

Don't you realize that your body is the temple of the Holy Spirit, who lives in you and was given to you by God? You do not belong to yourself.
– 1 Corinthians 6:19 NLT –

Do you want the power of the Holy Spirit to swell your life's sails? Well, be assured of the following:

Know that the Spirit lives in you (1 Cor. 3:16; 6:19): The Holy Spirit was given to the church of Christ (Rom. 8:9). He transforms you and other believers into temples of the Almighty. He changes your life into a temple of the living God.

Know that the Spirit is the Guarantee that you will reach the finish line (Eph. 1:13-14): The Spirit guarantees that a heavenly feast awaits you. He guarantees that you will reach the finish line safely because you believe in Christ. He also guarantees that He will be with you wherever you are on the road. He will make sure that you reach the eternal home of the Lord safely.

Let the Spirit fill your life every day (Eph. 5:18): Your life should be like an empty vessel that is filled with the Spirit each day. Be the clay in His hands for Him to model. Ask Him to fill the vessel of your life to the brim with life-giving water, enough to spill over to others.

Day 123

Your Life Story

"Surely the LORD is in this place."

– Genesis 28:16 NLT –

Can you recall Jacob's dream (Gen. 28:10-22)? He dreamt about a ladder and saw angels climbing up and down. All of a sudden God was there, too. He promised Jacob that He would be with him. Jacob then awoke and exclaimed in shock: "Surely the Lord is in this place, and I was not aware of it" (v. 16). What a mistake not to recognize the Lord when He is with you!

Fortunately, Jacob afterwards honored the Lord by marking the spot with a rock and naming the town Bethel, the House of God. In that way a very ordinary town suddenly became the residence of God, and Jacob, in turn, became a brand-new person!

Jacob's rock proclaimed God is here. By the way, do the stories of your life also reflect the presence of God? Is your life a holy shrine to His honor? Is your life a Bethel—a house of God? Do you realize that the Holy Spirit lives within you when you bow before Jesus? Dedicate your whole life to being the living house of God. Let your every word, every deed, every thought, shout it out—God is here! Bethel!

Day 124

The Voice of the Spirit

The LORD delights in every detail of their lives. Though they stumble, they will never fall, for the LORD holds them by the hand.

– Psalm 37:23-24 NLT –

God devised a wonderful plan to make sure that we never forget His name. He sent the Holy Spirit to all who follow Christ. Read Romans 8:15-16 to see how the Spirit does it: "You received the Spirit of sonship. And by Him we cry, Abba, Father. The Spirit Himself testifies with our spirit that we are God's children."

Listen carefully and you will hear the Holy Spirit in your heart calling to God lovingly and compassionately today. He is the inner voice that calls to our wonderful heavenly Father on our behalf! It is the task of the Holy Spirit to form an intimate, never-ending bond between you and God. He sees to it that you are always very close to God, even when you don't experience it!

Open your ears today and listen carefully so that you can hear His voice deep in your heart. Hear the Spirit conversing with God about you, calling out to the Father on your behalf. Allow the Spirit to give you the assurance that God is your Father, a loving Father who cares about every little detail of your life.

Day 125

Prime Time for God

Because of Christ and our faith in Him, we can now come boldly and confidently into God's presence.
– Ephesians 3:12 NLT –

Make time somewhere during the day to switch off your cell phone, close the door, be alone with God and read His Word. The Lord's Word is not merely letters on paper. While you read the Bible, the Holy Spirit is always at work burning these letters into your heart. The heavenly seeds that He sows in your heart while you dwell in His Word will quickly take root in your mind, as well as on your hands and feet.

The blessings you reap if you are prepared to invest time to seek the face of the Lord will be beyond belief, because every time you do this you find yourself in the Holy Spirit's sphere of power and attention. Every time you do this your life is molded to the glory of God by the most powerful person in the universe!

There are no shortcuts on the road to spiritual success; however, there are right roads! If you want to follow the main road of faith, one of the most important routes to take is that of setting aside special time for God each day. Oh yes, also dedicate the rest of the day to God as well! Do this every day.

Day 126

He Holds Me

In the same way, the Spirit helps us in our weakness. We do not know what we ought to pray for, but the Spirit Himself intercedes for us through wordless groans.

– Romans 8:26 NIV –

When Christ returned to heaven, He did not leave us to our own devices. He gave us the Holy Spirit in His place, as Helper, Consoler, Spiritual Assistant, Advocate, Savior, Intercessor, Builder of Temples…Now, we are no longer alone, even if no one else is present. The Holy Spirit is our permanent companion. He is with us all the time. He raises us up when we are really down and out. He intercedes for us with the Father when we do not know how or what to pray. He keeps us on the right spiritual path to the Father's heart.

When we start losing direction, the Holy Spirit immediately comes looking for us. When we try to hide from God in the darkness of our own faults, He switches on a bright spiritual light in our lives. We cannot run, we cannot hide—neither from ourselves nor from Him. The Spirit's task is to one day deliver us, safe and sound, to God the Father in His eternal heavenly dwelling (Eph. 1:13-14). This is why He consistently ensures that we stay on track. He keeps us en route to God.

DAY 127

World-Shakers

Because of Christ and our faith in Him, we can now come boldly and confidently into God's presence.
– Ephesians 3:12 NLT –

Being mindful is not self-indulgent. On the contrary, it is an inner awareness of God's amazing goodness that enhances our spiritual capacity for caring in our relationships with Him and others. We must escape our mindless routines. They often trap us in deadly habits and negative thought patterns that steal our passion and creativity. Only when we experience deep community with God through the work of His Holy Spirit, does life become more gracious and enriching.

The more we realize that we are truly filled with God's closeness through the work of the Holy Spirit, the more we become aware of His extraordinary grace and the privilege of being alive in His presence right this very moment. The more we cultivate our awareness of God's grace, the more we succeed in breaking free from our prisons of negativity and cynicism. As we experience God's peace, we begin to treat ourselves and others with more grace and dignity.

As we become more aware of God's hand in changing our world through Christ, we join His band of world-shakers who spread the good news of Christ everywhere they go.

Day 128

Not for Sale

Truly my soul finds rest in God; my salvation comes from Him. Truly He is my rock and my salvation.
– Psalm 62:1-2 NIV –

Two Simons...Simon the sorcerer and Simon Peter, in the town Samaria (Acts 8). Simon the sorcerer was known as "The Mighty;" the other Simon as Peter, the Rock, the one upon whose testimony Christ built His church (Matt. 16). Simon the powerhouse versus Simon the rock: worldly sorcery compared to heavenly power. No contest! Simon the sorcerer was immediately stumped when he saw how Peter communicated the gospel to people in Samaria. The power of the Spirit that worked through Peter changed their lives from the inside out. Then the sorcerer tried to purchase this supernatural power.

What a mistake to think that God can be purchased with money! The Spirit works in His own way. He is never for sale. His power cannot be copied. Thank God, He works charitably and completely free in the lives of those whom He changes into temples of the Almighty. The Spirit changes ordinary people into rocks who can bravely testify about Jesus, not into sorcerers who try to impress with tricks.

Let Him use you as one of His rocks, so that people around you may change in the right way, too.

Day 129

Standing in the Wind

Pray in the Spirit at all times and on every occasion. Stay alert and be persistent in your prayers for all believers everywhere.

– Ephesians 6:18 NLT –

The Day of Pentecost was not windless—anything but. On that day a mighty, heavenly gale-force wind of the Spirit started blowing through our dead and dying world. When the Holy Spirit came down on that day, His wind and fire gave new life to the entire church. People who had been scared before started speaking about Christ fearlessly all of a sudden. At every turn they found their tongues had been loosened. An abundance of power was available once again—supernatural power to witness, to sing, to serve, to make miracles happen!

The heavenly Wind of the Spirit is still blowing today. His power is no less now than it was on the Day of Pentecost—only you and I restrict His power. Perhaps we no longer believe that He has remained unchanged to this day, and that He will remain so forever after. Let us ask the Spirit to fill our souls once again (Eph. 5:17). Let us spread our sails to catch the Wind, the right Wind, the Wind of heaven!

If we stand in the Wind of the Spirit, we will boldly speak about our great God. Then this broken world of ours will be full of hope again: heavenly hope!

Day 130

Temples of God

Don't you realize that your body is the temple of the Holy Spirit, who lives in you and was given to you by God? You do not belong to yourself.

– 1 Corinthians 6:19 NLT –

Paul tells an unbelievable story in 1 Corinthians 6:19-20. He writes that we were bought by Jesus when we were still enslaved by sin and death. He came searching for us on the market square of sins. On that day His blood was the method of payment by which He made us His property. Isn't it unbelievable that Jesus has such abundant love for the wrong people, for sinners such as you and me? Well, that is precisely what Christ is like. That is why He buys sinners, even today. His specialty is saving the broken and the dead.

There is another important thing that Jesus did when He bought us. According to 1 Corinthians 6:19, He gave us over to the lifelong care of the Holy Spirit. There and then the Holy Spirit transformed us into temples of the living God. Now we are His final earthly home before the Second Coming. The Spirit builds living temples in honor of our Father. He transforms us into living dwellings in which God can live and work.

We have been set apart permanently to reflect God's greatness. Therefore, we have to live up to, speak up to and do up to His great name! Let's do it!

Day 131

How Far Is God?

The LORD replied, "My Presence will go with you, and I will give you rest."

– Exodus 33:14 NIV –

"How far from us is God really, Sir?" a little girl asked me recently. "Why do you want to know?" I asked. "Well, my mom and dad say I am wasting my time praying to God because He is too far away to hear," she answered.

"No, He is not far. I had a conversation with Him a few minutes ago," I immediately responded. "In fact, God is always only one prayer away." "All distance disappears in the exact place where you and I bow down before God and talk to Him in the name of Jesus. Then God is right there—a mere prayer away! We never have to shout, or use a loudspeaker to talk to Him, because He is not deaf. Neither do you have to use big and difficult words, or say long prayers. All God wants from us is sincerity. He is interested in the language of your heart. That is all."

"I agree, because I know that God is always close to me. It seems that my parents have become blind to His presence," the girl remarked with sadness in her voice, walking away.

Day 132

Omnipotence

"And surely I am with you always, to the very end of the age."

– Matthew 28:20 NIV –

Nothing can ever separate you from God's love—not even the biggest crisis you have to face. Nothing in life is a match for the power and love of God, absolutely nothing. Paul assures us of this amazing fact in Romans 8:31-39. You are the special property of the Lord because you believe in Christ. You are so precious to Him that He carries you in the palm of His almighty hand night and day. You are never alone, not for a single moment.

Even though you may feel defenseless and weak at times, you are still a member of God's winning team. Eternity has a permanent place in your heart. You are on your way to the heavenly winning post. Keep on believing that. Do not allow your emotions to play games with you. The Lord is not far from you merely because you feel that way. The Word promises that God is always near.

Although you may feel that the prayers you send up get stuck at ceiling height, you must know that it is your feelings running away with you once again. God is omnipotent—He is with you. Believe it and be free!

Day 133

Ever-Present

God is our refuge and strength, an ever-present help in trouble.

– Psalm 46:1 NIV –

Sometimes we are in the presence of VIPs without even realizing it. Think of Jacob. Do you remember when he was fleeing from Esau and he spent one night sleeping with his head against a rock? The Lord unexpectedly appeared to him in a dream. Afterwards, rather shocked, Jacob confessed, "The Lord is in this place, and I didn't even realize it."

The biggest mistake you could ever make is not recognizing the Lord when He is with you. That would be allowing the opportunity of a lifetime to slip through your fingers! And who knows, maybe you are going to cross paths with a few famous people this year. But the most important person of all is God Himself. You will see His heavenly fingerprints in many places around you.

Don't ignore the Lord. Don't wait until He awakens you from your dreams before you realize that He is present! Make God the Guest of Honor in your life every single day.

Day 134

From Chaos to Calm

God is our refuge and strength, an ever-present help in trouble.

– Psalm 46:1 NIV –

In one moment even the stormiest seas can become calm. In the blink of an eye huge storms can abate. The same can also happen in your life. Chaos can instantaneously make room for peace. Noise can be replaced by soft silence in an instant. Unrest can be chased away by heavenly peace. How? Just realize afresh that the Lord is God. He alone! Believe the Word that the Lord is with you right there in the storm. Believe the Word that He is the only hiding place in time of danger.

Subside. Calm down. Come to rest. Let your heart become still and calm. Let your turbulent mood find a hiding place at the Lord's feet. Look up. Notice the Lord, high over nations and far above the dead gods of this world. See Him in faith. Bow gently before Him in the name of Jesus. Kneel in worship.

Know that the Lord is the Almighty. He has all power in His hands. He alone is Lord, only He. He is your only Hope, your only Savior. Notice Him, and come to rest in His presence. Look up to Him and experience His heavenly peace.

Day 135

Wake Up!

"The LORD your God is with you, the Mighty Warrior who saves. He will take great delight in you; in His love He will no longer rebuke you, but will rejoice over you with singing."

– Zephaniah 3:17 NIV –

Do you live in a make-believe world? If so, open your eyes! Leave all your unfulfilled dreams behind, because the Lord's heavenly ladder extends down into your life today. God's plan for your life will turn into reality. As you deliberately begin to live your life in His company from now on, you'll become aware that you walk on holy ground every day. You will realize that you are in the presence of the One who holds heaven and earth in the palm of His hand. What a privilege to know that the most powerful Person in the universe accompanies you wherever you go.

Maybe you will come across a few important public figures in the course of your life, but the most important One, who is with you right now, is the living God. He is always close to you, whether you are among believers and friends, at work, or at home. Be grateful that God honors you with His personal presence! Bow down before Him. From now on invite Him every day to be the Guest of Honor in your life!

Day 136

By Your Side

"No one can snatch them away from Me, for My Father has given them to Me, and He is more powerful than anyone else. No one can snatch them from the Father's hand."

– John 10:28-29 NLT –

Nothing shall separate you from the love of Christ if you know Jesus as the Lord and sole Ruler of your life. This truth is shared by Paul in such a compelling manner in Romans 8:31-39. You are God's precious property because Christ wrote your name in the Book of Life. Every day you, together with all of God's children, fit neatly into the palm of His hand. You are God's sole property, bought and sealed by His Spirit.

Even when you are weak, you are still God's property. You are somebody with eternity in your heart. You are en route to the winning post. Believe it. Don't ever allow your emotions to play games with you. You are not far away from God merely because it sometimes feels that way. The Gospels state that God is always near.

If you think that your prayers do not rise above the roof of your home, it is merely your emotions fooling you. God is everywhere—all around you. Stop trying to find God in the distance. He is close by. Believe it and be free!

Day 137

A New Song

Sing to the LORD a new song; sing to the LORD, all the earth.

– Psalm 96:1 NIV –

Paul and Silas held a celebration in a jail in Philippi (Acts 16) one night. Do you remember how the two of them were cruelly assaulted and beaten to a pulp earlier that same day? Afterwards, they were thrown into the maximum-security cell of Philippi's stinking jail. At midnight, Paul decided to sing. It was not hate songs against their enemies. They did not ask for those who assaulted them to be punished by God. Nothing of the sort. All that was on the lips of Paul and Silas was praise for God.

With bloodied bodies and false voices, they sent the purest sounds imaginable to God. Paul and Silas wouldn't have won an Idols' competition that night, but their sincerity to bring God praise under the worst imaginable circumstances touched God's heart. That's why the earth suddenly started shaking.

It is about time that we as followers of Jesus started singing different songs. All too easily we join the choirs of the discouraged. We constantly listen to hit parades where hate songs and inflammatory lyrics have the upper hand. Let's learn from Paul that true hit music is praise to God.

Day 138

God Is Great

Commit everything you do to the Lord. Trust Him, and He will help you.

– Psalm 37:5 NLT –

At times I am very aware of my weaknesses. When I trip over a stone on the road of life, I realize that I am fragile. Yes, when all is said and done, I am no more than dust and wind. Even so, this fragile old clay pot contains a precious Treasure. Truly, I am never alone. The Lord is with me because Jesus is the Lord of my life. God is my constant and only Wealth, my Gold, my Silver, my Life.

Even when I am small, God is great. When I am weak, God is infinitely strong. Every time I falter, God is my Rock. When I fall, God remains the strong One. What a miracle: small and LARGE together forever—the weak me and Almighty God! What an act of grace to have been made a child of our heavenly Father by Christ. He is the One who catches me every time I fall. I know that God never leaves me on my own. He bends down to pick me up, exactly as Psalm 37 promises.

Therefore, I can walk straight ahead until the end because I am accompanied by the strongest One in the universe: Almighty God.

Day 139

Carrying the Flag

Light shines on the righteous and joy on the upright in heart. Rejoice in the LORD, you who are righteous, and praise His holy name.

– Psalm 97:11-12 NIV –

I once read a story about two armies who entered into battle in the American War of Independence. One of the generals, realizing that his soldiers were losing badly, ordered them all to fall back immediately. But the flag bearer right at the front refused. In haste, the general asked a messenger to go and instruct the man to fall back immediately. But the flag bearer refused once again. Then he sent back the following message to the general, "No, Sir, I'm not falling back. Please instruct the soldiers to march forward to me!"

We are the flag bearers of the gospel. Often you and I find ourselves alone on hostile territory. Perhaps we all feel like falling back then. Don't! Instead, call fellow believers through your actions and words to join you at the front, there where you are on point duty for the Lord.

Plant the flag of the gospel right at the front in His honor. Be strong for the Lord. You are never alone in any event. The One who is stronger is with you. The Lord controls every trench on the battlefield, each piece of ground where you may find yourself.

Day 140

The True Facts

"I'll be with you as you do this, day after day after day, right up to the end of the age."
– Matthew 28:20 THE MESSAGE –

"The Lord doesn't care about me anymore. Why does He let all these terrible things happen to me?" Have you ever said words like these? Or have you thought it perhaps? Of course you are not alone if you feel like this sometimes. Many people have the same thoughts.

What are the true facts? Well, may I remind you of Jesus' last words on earth, a few minutes before His departure to heaven: He assured us that He would be with us until the end of time. Jesus will never, ever leave us—we are too precious to Him. He will accompany everyone who believes in Him to the end of the road.

Are you going to join all the grumblers of the world who complain, "No one's burden is as heavy as mine," or are you going to see the Lord who holds you safely in His hands today?

Day 141

Sharing Yourself

Don't forget to do good and to share with those in need. These are the sacrifices that please God.
— Hebrews 13:16 NLT —

Relationships require far more than just exchanging information with each other. Not too long ago I had to do strategic planning with a church council. I soon realized that few people, who had been serving on the council for more than ten years, knew very much about one another. They were actually still complete strangers who merely had meetings together. And then as a team they had to make important decisions about the Lord's work!

Relationships are not merely a case of knowing all the answers to questions like what job someone does, how many children they have and where they spend their holidays. That is information. Real relationships mean sharing a part of your life with another person. No, it means sharing yourself. Real relationships happen when you and someone else start sharing the same heartbeat.

Relationships require you to be someone's tower of strength. It requires time, sacrifice and honesty. And prayer on a regular basis. Real relationships always require a lot. You have to calculate the price of friendship well, because you put your life on the line for a friend. Just ask Jesus!

Day 142

Friendship

Two are better than one...if either of them falls down, one can help the other up.

– Ecclesiastes 4:9-10 NIV –

Maybe you know the expression that you should write the bad things your friends do to you in sand, but the good things they do for you should be engraved in stone. Wise words! The wind blows sand away so easily, but the wind cannot accomplish much against stone. Beware of not holding little things against your loved ones, or you may lose them. Take a back seat. Do as the Bible says: Forgive. Reach out and offer a helping hand. Be willing to start over.

When you lose a friend, you have really lost a lot. This kind of loss is immeasurable. Don't allow it to happen. A good friend is worth much more than gold. Every friend is a gift from the Lord to enrich and fulfill your life.

Never neglect your friends. Pray for them regularly and spend time with them. Make them aware that they are special and precious to you. Protect their good names and listen to their sound advice. Support and help them when they stumble and fall. Do everything in your power to be a one-of-a-kind friend.

Day 143

Counting Your Blessings

Be gentle with one another, sensitive. Forgive one another as quickly and thoroughly as God in Christ forgave you.

– Ephesians 4:32 The Message –

What does your balance sheet for this year look like so far? Did you use all the chances you were given? Were you more softhearted—someone who cared more about others? Did you show more compassion; a hand more open to those in need? Was your tongue coated in silver more often than it was full of venom? Were you more faithful in prayer? Perhaps you got to know God's Word a little better? Were the lives of others enriched by your friendship? Were you a neighbor to someone whom life had knocked down? Were you the one who made a positive, heavenly difference in the lives of others?

Have you enjoyed this year so far, despite the hardship around you? Have you really noticed the sunrise? Have you listened to the voices of children playing happily? Did you feel your minister's sermon on a Sunday morning was meant for you in particular? Did you leave church with a smile on your face because you realized God truly loves you? Well, if these moments of happiness on your balance sheet top the heartache, then it has been a good year so far.

Day 144

Editing Life

Friends come and friends go, but a true friend sticks by you like family.

– Proverbs 18:24 THE MESSAGE –

Each of us needs to be in a healthy growth-oriented relationship with someone else who "edits" us to make the right impact for God. We aren't islands! We need each other's constant advice, shaping, intercessory prayer, exhortation, and encouragement. If you don't have someone like this in your life, it's about time! Pray that God will send the right person to assist you in your spiritual growth. Be specific: Ask the Lord to make you transparent so that the right mentor will easily find you.

By the way, how many people are you also mentoring at present? In whose lives are you investing some of God's good gifts on a daily or a weekly basis? Listen, you really need to be a mentor for someone else. You need to constantly share what you've received from God. Become a "publisher" for at least one other person who is busy writing a good story to honor God with his/her life. Pray today that God will show you exactly who it is that you need to "edit" to serve God and others more effectively. As a follower of Christ you must actively influence and encourage people around you to live godly lives.

DAY 145

A High Price

"If you try to hang on to your life, you will lose it. But if you give up your life for My sake, you will save it."

– Matthew 16:25 NLT –

You've heard of Maximilian Kolbe, the Franciscan priest who was incarcerated in Auschwitz during the Second World War. After an inmate escaped, as was the rule, 10 prisoners were chosen to die in his place. One of them had a wife and children, and Kolbe volunteered to take the man's place and face a torturous death. It took two weeks for him to die, when he was given a lethal injection of acid.

Kolbe's actions remind me of the words of Jesus that there is no greater love than when someone is prepared to lay down his life for his friends!

What do we ever sacrifice for one another? Whose lives have been enriched by us? Who knows, maybe our faith is far too safe and boring!

DAY 146

Relationships Matter

The LORD has done great things for us, and we are filled with joy.

– Psalm 126:3 NIV –

Joy comes in small portions—like that cup of coffee you share with a friend. Or in the unplanned visit with someone you meet. Life is all about relationships. Did you know that your mind was created to make decisions regarding people almost one tenth of a second faster than decisions about other things. A recent study found that when we are relaxed and not doing anything, our brain is most probably busy taking a closer look at our relationships.

The Lord created us to love. We are wired for relationships. We are designed to be able to experience deep feelings of compassion and love. Don't become a slave to full schedules, meetings and activities. Your faith must be relation-driven, not task-driven. Your faith is not all about the things that you do for the Lord, but also about the relationships you build.

It is about good things that you do for people with real names and addresses. Be there for the people close to you. But also be there for the strangers who may cross your path unexpectedly.

Day 147

The Speed of Sound

Teach us to number our days, that we may gain a heart of wisdom.

– Psalm 90:12 NIV –

Time is money. There's no time for lounging around and doing nothing. No wonder we have phrases like "time management" or "effective use of time." Nowadays we even need to learn how to save time to be effective! There you have it: We're time addicts! We constantly run around at the speed of light to every new demand, in the hope that we'll save two or three minutes somewhere. If we do, we immediately forget about the "saved time" when we arrive anxiously and tired at our destination.

No, we don't really save time. We just chase up our heart rate and heap loads of stress on our shoulders through our hectic daily pace of life. This is because we're chasing after wind and dust storms. The Lord doesn't intend for us to live like this. It's not part of His plan that we live at the speed of light every day. We were made for relationships. And we need time for these—time to stand still, time to take hands.

Well, do you ever have time for that? Do you have the courage to reduce your speed-of-light lifestyle to walking pace? Then you'll start experiencing God and others again.

Day 148

Built for Relationships

*Do nothing out of selfish ambition or vain conceit.
Rather, in humility value others above yourselves.*
– Philippians 2:3 NIV –

Genesis 2 tells us that there was trouble in the Garden of Eden, of all places. The reason: Adam was home alone and relationship hungry! He couldn't find a soul mate. God said this was not good, since man was not made to be alone.

All these "Rambo" figures that take on the world alone might be Hollywood's idea of success, but it's false. No human is an island. We're built for relationships. We long for God and other people. We want to cherish and love. Our hearts remain restless until we find rest in the arms of God, but also in the closeness of others.

From His side, God also yearns for a living relationship with everyone bearing His signature. We are His artwork, His personal property. We are the highlight of His beautiful creation. That's why He sent His Son to look for us when we were lost in the dark. When we wandered the farthest from Him, Jesus came, caught up with us, and accompanied us back to the Garden. By the way, there's still some space left in Paradise Street. Move back there immediately, back into the relationship where you belong!

Day 149

The New Big

"Whoever wants to become great among you must be your servant, and whoever wants to be first must be slave of all."

– Mark 10:43-44 NIV –

"Small is the new big." Small is important. It's so important that it overtook big recently! When small is present in church, relationships are more personal. Small is also closer. Small is...more effective. Small is face-to-face. Small is not as expensive. Small is faster. That's why small is the new big thing in relationships. Success and big/large/extra-large were too close for too long. Success was correlated with large numbers, huge crowds, abundant resources, colossal incomes... those days are gone. They should never have existed in church in the first place. It's now the turn of small.

Small churches, small Bible studies, small gatherings, small services, small outreaches, small discussions, small prayers...that's what really changes the world. Just read the Gospels again. Jesus was into small. Jesus loved individuals. That's why He spent so much time with His group of 12 disciples or with outcasts. Jesus was big on small. He had all the time in the world to care for individuals. He did relationships at the speed of one person at a time.

DAY 150

Mile Three

"If anyone forces you to go one mile, go with them two miles."

– Matthew 5:41 NIV –

In his amazing book *The Orthodox Heretic*, Peter Rollins tells the story of a man who listened to Jesus' Sermon on the Mount (Matt. 5-7). He was captivated when Jesus said that we need to walk a second mile for our enemies. Later, this man encountered a Roman soldier and offered to carry his weapons for two miles instead of the one mile that Roman law required. Some time later he met Jesus again, and told Him that he practically applied his "two-mile law." Immediately Jesus told the man that he had misunderstood and that it was actually three miles!

What is the point of this story? Jesus didn't simply come to bring a new set of rules. For Him, it is all about new relationships that are driven by love. No, the Ten Commandments did not expire (vv. 17-20). Jesus just clarifies that the original meaning of these was to live in fresh new relationships with God and others. The law is not a bunch of dos and don'ts.

The question is: Are we successful at walking extra miles at all? Do we truly understand what Jesus means when He tells us to add a mile or two on every route with our enemies?

DAY 151
Chasing Fear Away

"Have I not commanded you? Be strong and courageous. Do not be afraid; do not be discouraged, for the LORD your God will be with you wherever you go."

– Joshua 1:9 NIV –

Elie Wiesel, a Romanian-born Jewish American, Holocaust survivor and Nobel Peace Prize winner, tells the story of his visit to a Jewish community during the reign of the old communistic regime in Moscow. During a religious feast, some of them openly danced in the streets. When asked why they were dancing, a woman answered: "All year I live in fear. But once a year, on this day, I refuse to be afraid. Then I'm a Jew and I dance in the streets!" We should also learn how to dance. We live in times where fear is one of the dominant emotions for many of us. Tragic, or what!

Did you know that we're born with only two basic fears? The fear of loud noises and the fear of falling. Still, many adults now have hundreds of fears. That's why we need to learn anew how to celebrate, not just once a year, but every day. Our identity is anchored in the Lord, who is infinitely bigger than the biggest of our fears. Jesus is our Lord. Thus, we can dance and sing, even with tears on our cheeks…we can be glad and call the bluff of every old or new fear that threatens us.

Day 152

God Walks Quietly

I know the Lord is always with me. I will not be shaken, for He is right beside me.

– Psalm 16:8 NLT –

Simply by speaking, God can quiet a violent storm in an instant! Just ask the seafarers in Psalm 107. One day they saw the calm sea around them suddenly turn into violent waves; their boat rolled to and fro uncontrollably. They realized that they were in serious trouble. There and then they started to pray. All at once, God performed a miracle. He calmed the waters; something He likes to do! God addressed the giant waves to calm down when His people started to pray.

Still today, the Lord walks quietly on stormy waters. The most powerful winds cannot blow Him off course, especially not when His children flounder helplessly in dangerous storms.

Even when the winds are at their strongest, the Lord calmly reaches out to His people. He knows when they feel trapped and helpless. He knows their feelings of fear and despair when giant waves wash over their lifeboats. When they anxiously call for help He hears every word. He will constrain the winds that blow all round them at once. In no time He will clear the dark clouds that have gathered above them. He will also do it today. All you have to do is ask!

Day 153

Math

If God is for us, who can be against us?
– Romans 8:31 NIV –

Are you afraid of the dark? Does that small portion of life that is yours to live every day get you down? Well, then you have to do the right thing: Pray! Ask God to open your eyes wide for a change. Start doing heavenly math. That will make you realize that ONE plus one is a winning recipe!

Take Elisha, when he was surrounded by the Arameans (2 Kings 6). The one morning his servant got up and feared for their lives. Elisha asked God to open his servant's eyes, but still he could see nothing else than the Arameans on all sides. He was paralyzed with fear.

Elisha's words, "Those who are with us are more than those who are with them," did not help. According to the servant's arithmetic, one plus one made two, and that was far less than the army that surrounded them—until God opened his eyes. Only then did the servant understand heavenly mathematics. He discovered that ONE plus one is always the majority when that ONE is God. With God on your side, you are a winner. With Him on your side, you will always be the majority.

Day 154

"I Ain't Afraid"

For the Spirit God gave us does not make us timid, but gives us power, love and self-discipline.
– 2 Timothy 1:7 NIV –

You may know the song from the *Ghostbusters* movies—"I ain't afraid of no ghost." Well, we bump into ghosts all the time. We are constantly haunted by our own fears. A shocking piece of research states that the older we get, the more our brains form synaptic links that are related to fear. Why? Is it because life is so dangerous or because people are so toxic?

Perhaps we continue to live on the fringes of our own lives...those fringes where fear reigns unchallenged. Freedom begins when I encounter my inner fears. How? There's no quick answer. But one way is to listen to my inner self-talk. An awareness of my inner discussions will bring me into contact with my fears. Then I'll begin to see them for what they really are—pale ghosts!

God's freedom is always an inner freedom. The freedom that the Spirit brings moves me away from the fringes of my life to my inner self. His freedom lets me discover the true me. Only then will I grasp His freedom that sets people free. That's when I sing, "I ain't afraid of no ghost."

Day 155

In God's Hands

"I know you well and you are special to Me."
– Exodus 33:12 The Message –

Asaph, one of the believers in the Bible who always went against the tide, wrote in Psalm 73:13 that he had been near to losing his faith after he had seen the prosperity of wicked people compared to his own suffering. Fortunately, the Lord opened his eyes to see what it was all about (v. 17). Asaph came to realize that God deals with sinners in His own way (vv. 18-20). He also learnt that the Lord never forsakes His children. God is the Rock where people who are afraid can hide (v. 23). Listen to Asaph's words, "My flesh and my heart may fail, but God is the strength of my heart and my portion forever" (v. 26 NIV).

The Lord will never forsake us, not even when we are in revolt against Him. That is why Asaph confesses, "When my heart was grieved and my spirit embittered, I was senseless and ignorant; I was a brute beast before You. Yet I am always with You; You hold me by my right hand" (vv. 21-23 NIV).

Well, there you have it—the true facts! Do you believe it? Or do you listen to all the noise in your head?

DAY 156

God's Protection

The Lord protects all those who love Him.
– Psalm 145:20 nlt –

There are far more Scripture verses in the Bible that say God protects us *in* danger than *from* danger. The Lord does not necessarily safeguard us from all crises, but He does guarantee His presence in the midst of every storm. God doesn't allow us to take shelter in "safe harbors" all the time.

He does not automatically guarantee safety, good weather and sunshine. He wants to teach us to walk with Christ in our storms. That is why the Bible often says that we should seek the Lord in times of affliction. He is our only rock when the storms are raging. He is our steady anchor when the winds are howling. He is present in the storm and always on duty!

When we find ourselves in a crisis, then we have to be the first line of prayer defense. We must call on the Lord, not our minister, or some or other prayer chain. It is always good if others pray for us during these times, but the Lord commands us to talk to Him during times of crisis. That is the ABC of any Storm Survival Strategy. Do it! God will give deliverance in His own way.

Day 157

God Knows

"He pays even greater attention to you, down to the last detail—even numbering the hairs on your head!"

– Matthew 10:30 THE MESSAGE –

Having read Matthew 10:30, which says that God even counts every hair on our heads, I told my bald-headed friend that he was really making the Lord's task easy. There is nothing left to count on his head!

God is so near, so intensely involved with us that He makes time to get to know the detail of our lives. So much so that He is up to date with "unimportant" details, such as when we lose a hair. Even if you are privileged enough to have a good head of hair, how many did you lose during the night? God knows. His care is so sincere that He knows even that! How about that for attention to detail? How about that for intense awareness and priority treatment!

God takes special care of His prized earthly possessions. We, who have been bought through the blood of His Son, are His family, His handiwork, His property. That is why He nurtures and looks after us. That is why He carries and protects us. So, touch your hair (or your head!) and know that God is near. Then bow before Him in deep reverence.

Day 158

His Wings

Whoever dwells in the shelter of the Most High will rest in the shadow of the Almighty.

– Psalm 91:1 NIV –

God always knows where you are. He watches your movements closely, 24/7. He can trace you in no time at all, wherever you might be wandering. Each earthly address where you spend your time is recorded in the heavenly books. You will never be able to change your address on the quiet without God discovering it in a divine instant. That is why He knows full well when you land in real storms. You can be sure that He will be there in the blink of an eye.

Always know that when you feel caught up among giant waves, the Lord is very close to you. You are too precious for Him to allow gales to blow you away from Him. You are one of God's very special possessions, and He will speak out to calm the storms round you. He will protect you. Ask Him to do it!

Remember to bow to Him in thankfulness afterwards. Honor Him for being with you in your dark hour of need. Worship the only Lord who can change even the most intense darkness, surrounding you with the brightest light, turning your night into day!

Day 159

Get Out of the Boat

Jesus immediately said to them: "Take courage! It is I. Don't be afraid."

– Matthew 14:27 NIV –

To walk on water is not normal. Ask Peter! You have to climb out of your boat before you can walk on water with Jesus. And that requires a fixed stare in His direction and a secure grasp of His hand. But is walking on water really as difficult as some people think. Yes and no! Yes, walking on water is difficult for those unused to doing so!

For those who never risk talking about their faith proactively, or who never stay obedient to God through thick and thin, life's storms can be devastating. But for those who time and time again risk following Jesus even in the midst of a storm, and who are not embarrassed to be carriers of the cross, sometimes they walk on water. It does not scare them. It is also not impossible.

Jesus lifts us above every storm, provided that we place our hand in His! Don't let life's storms cause you to let go of His hand. Look past your crises—look towards Him, who is greater! Walk towards Him. That is the secret.

DAY 160

A Safe Haven

The heartfelt counsel of a friend is as sweet as perfume and incense.

– Proverbs 27:9 NLT –

It seems to me that safe people are as scarce as safe places. Who or what is a safe person? It is someone in whose presence you can open your heart. It is someone with whom you can just be yourself without fearing that he or she will use it against you. A safe person will always protect your integrity in front of others—and always enjoys speaking to God about you.

Shedding tears is a gift from God to wash our insides clean of hurt and pain. But our tears are not safe with everyone. Some see it as a sign of weakness, or an inability to stare life bravely in the face. How great that the Lord made some people so free that they are safe havens for those around them. With these folks you can be fragile and broken. And even sensitive. In their presence you find healing for your tired soul.

Do you know safe people? Cherish them! Thank God over and over for them. Are you someone like this? Not? Then get to know Romans 12—learn how to mourn with those who are mourning and to rejoice with those who are rejoicing. There you will also learn how to associate with the humble and to dry the tears of others.

Day 161

More than Enough

Let us not become weary in doing good, for at the proper time we will reap a harvest if we do not give up.

– Galatians 6:9 NIV –

Our basic needs are to have food and clothes every day. Our foremost need is to have our dreams come true. That is what the clever guys tell us.

Well, the Bible tells me that Christ has come to fulfill our basic needs. John 6 says Jesus is the Bread of Life. He takes away our hunger forever. Christ also fulfills our foremost needs. John 7 says that rivers of living water flow from us when we believe in Him. He lets us experience abundance every day. We who believe are blessed with armfuls of heavenly life of the kind that never comes to an end. Christ showers us with so many blessings each day that they overflow from our hands, feet and lips to others.

Christ is our everything! We lack for nothing. When life is dark, He is our Light. When we are surrounded by pain and disappointment, He is our Helper. When we feel we cannot or do not want to carry on, He is our heavenly Source of Strength. When we are abandoned by everybody, He stays near. When storms rage around us, He walks on the water beside us. Truly, we have more than we need, now and for always.

Day 162

Getting By

"Your Father knows what you need before you ask Him."

– Matthew 6:8 NIV –

One of the greatest sources of stress to ordinary salaried people is whether their hard-earned money is going to last until the end of the month. Is this your worst headache, too? Perhaps you are feeling like the person who told me the other day, "I wish I could afford living the way I do." To millions, life is a struggle for survival. Well, I have some "irrelevant" news for you: Christ says in Matthew 6 that God provides everything His children need in life. He knows our basic needs, but more than that, He knows what we need and when we need it.

God is always on time. Why would some believers find this news irrelevant? Because they do not really believe it. They work their fingers to the bone, thinking that their survival rests with them alone. They worry, as if Jesus did not intend God's promise to apply in the third millennium. They build their own futures as if God knows nothing of tomorrow.

What about you? Is this news irrelevant to you, or do you believe it? Well, if you do, be a bit more carefree about life than you were yesterday and the day before.

Day 163

Favor

The LORD will withhold no good thing from those who do what is right.

– Psalm 84:11 NLT –

Let's be honest—it is wonderful to be the blue-eyed boy and to receive preferential treatment now and then. It makes you feel very special. Well, God treats all of us that way when we follow Jesus. He calls us His children. That is what Paul writes in Romans 8. We are no longer slaves who are afraid or cautious of our ill-tempered owner. We are children of the King who lives in the house of the Lord every day. He is our Father. He is close to us. In addition, He covers us with His kindness from head to toe.

God promises many times in the Bible that He will provide our daily needs. And yet most of us have cupboards overflowing with meat, vegetables and other delicacies. Not even the rising prices and high inflation have caused us to go without food or with only dry bread as a staple food. To top it all, there is more than enough food and clothing for many days to come in most of our houses.

It seems to me that the Lord is favoring us. Why then are we complaining while we enjoy so much abundance? Isn't that blatant ingratitude?

Day 164

Out of Control

Be still in the presence of the LORD, and wait patiently for Him to act.

– Psalm 37:7 NLT –

I once read about a young British pastor who had a congregation of more than a thousand people in London about 200 years ago. He worked himself to death to keep them happy. At the age of 29 he had a fatal heart attack. On his deathbed this talented young man said that God had given him a Bible and a horse. Now he had worked his horse to death…what did it achieve? God needs healthy people, not people who work their horses to death and then have little energy left for His service because their health has failed.

If your life is in chaos, it is not caused by your boss, activities, schedule, diary, or your studies. You are the cause thereof. Don't point fingers elsewhere. You make that fatal decision every day to work yourself to the bone. You are not a victim or a passive observer of your busy life. You alone choose to follow that path! Nobody else forces you to damage your body.

Slow down. Realize that God is the God of your life. He will provide your needs.

Day 165

Two Loaves of Bread

"Therefore do not worry about tomorrow, for tomorrow will worry about itself. Each day has enough trouble of its own."

– Matthew 6:34 NIV –

One day, someone told me that the future looked very bleak indeed. I asked him: "What future are you talking about? The future a week from now, or the future in a year's time or in ten years' time? Because at the moment we are right in the middle of exactly that future about which we worried so much about ten years ago!" Despite that, all of us are surviving somehow! We are living last year and last week's future, here and now! Today is yesterday's tomorrow that we worried ourselves sick about. Incredible? No, it is grace! It is all thanks to God! He is true to His Word! He has cared for us exactly as He promised!

Can you recall how you worried about your future a few years back? Well, that future has arrived. Are you without food today? Not? Do you have enough warm blankets for tonight? Yes! Will you have enough money and supplies for the next month or so? Undoubtedly! Will you make it through the next year? Definitely! Now tell me, what are you worried about? To worry is nothing but a vote of no confidence in your heavenly Father!

Day 166
The Price Tag

Jesus said, "I am the Road, also the Truth, also the Life. No one gets to the Father apart from Me."
– John 14:6 THE MESSAGE –

The road to heaven has been irreparably damaged. Sin is the cause. We can't get back to heaven on our own. Not even the nicest things we do are sufficient or enough to create a new stairway to heaven. Every ladder that we erect is based on precarious foundations!

We need somebody to bridge this divide between God and us. If somebody does not build a path from heaven back to earth, we would be in a quandary. Somebody who is very powerful, big, strong and merciful has to help us. Fortunately there is such a person, just one—Jesus! He has already bridged the divide. Where no road existed before, He has built a road with His own life. His journey to us was the most expensive road in the universe. It opened a new road to God, a road with protection against sin and death.

If you are worried about the travel costs—Jesus has already purchased and paid for the ticket for your journey. Believe in Him as God over your life and just stay on His track daily.

Day 167

In His Hands

"So don't worry about tomorrow, for tomorrow will bring its own worries. Today's trouble is enough for today."

– Matthew 6:34 NLT –

I don't know what the future holds, but I do know who holds it! Do you believe that? If you do, you should live differently today. Why? Because tomorrow's uncertainties cannot and will not happen without God's knowledge. When tomorrow arrives, He will be there. He will report for duty, just like every other day. God will definitely be on time for tomorrow. Even if unexpected problems arise, if bad things like illness or crime come knocking at your door, God will not be absent. He will not be too busy with other urgent matters.

Your life does not escape God's attention for a single moment. Did you hear: Your life will not escape His attention ever! He didn't forget about you yesterday, it will not happen today, and He will not forget about you in the future. God holds you, also your times, seasons and years. Believe this, and live with a light heart.

Live joyously in God's abundant love.

DAY 168

Promotion

"Do not store up for yourselves treasures on earth, where moths and vermin destroy, and where thieves break in and steal. But store up for yourselves treasures in heaven."

– Matthew 6:19-20 NIV –

For many people promotion means only one thing— *more stuff*!...*more* money, *more* tangible benefits, *more* houses, *more* cars, *more* vacations, *more* status... For followers of Jesus, the word "promotion" should mean something completely different. It can't equate to more tangible things. Promotion should rather mean to grab every opportunity that the Lord offers you, sacrificing your valuable time and energy in His service.

The right type of promotion in God's service is to cast aside all the construction plans for your own little earthly kingdom, and to exchange them for the privilege of being a daily blessing to other people. True promotion is to be part of the lifelong adventure of building God's kingdom. This yields dividends that have eternal value. Promotion in God's kingdom becomes visible when you spend more time at the Lord's feet; when you make more time for the poor and the lonely; when you do more kind things for others; and also when you worry less about yourself and your own temporary needs.

Day 169

A Safe Refuge

The Lord is good, a refuge in times of trouble. He cares for those who trust in Him.

– Nahum 1:7 NIV –

Trouble! We know all about it. We experience it sometimes in our lives. Quite often it is our best friend for too long. Well, don't take it any longer. At the least, don't be victims of trouble. Do not slide into a "pity me, please" attitude. Take care that you never sing the evergreen theme song, "no one knows the troubles I feel."

Choose to effectively and correctly handle your troubles. Discuss them with God regularly. Pray! Seek His countenance until He opens up heaven above you. Do not let go of His hand when you are walking in darkness. Persevere to the end. A green pasture awaits you at the end of each troublesome event. That is what Psalm 23 promises. In effect, trouble is the shortcut on the right way to where you are heading.

Fortunately, the Shepherd of your life is accompanying you and seeing you through all your troubles while you search for better pastures. From now on, give your troubles a hard time when they want to rob you of your happiness. See to it that you and the Good Shepherd, Jesus Christ, walk side-by-side always. Note how His footprints cover all your problems.

Day 170

Don't Be an Addict

Anyone who competes as an athlete does not receive the victor's crown except by competing according to the rules.

– 2 Timothy 2:5 NIV –

There is a difference between a few busy seasons in your life and a program that is permanently filled to capacity. In everybody's life there are busy periods, but if it happens every day, then something is wrong!

Workaholism has become a socially acceptable illness—everybody does it. When do you have this terrible disease? Well, when it robs you of precious time that you should have spent with God. Or when it alienates you from your loved ones.

When you have no time left for God, for others, or for yourself, then you are addicted to your work. When you collapse dead tired into bed every evening...just to wake up tired the next morning and begin rushing again, then you are held captive by your work.

Listen up: it is not just a bad habit to be hurried all the time, it is a sin. You are living outside God's will because you are living outside the speed limits that He determined for your body. Trust God to give you what you need daily (Matt. 6:25-34). Show that you believe it, by living at a slower pace!

Day 171

Tough Times

God is faithful; He will not let you be tempted beyond what you can bear. But when you are tempted, He will also provide a way out so that you can endure it.

– 1 Corinthians 10:13 NIV –

"This isn't fair. I have been serving the Lord for years, but now everything in my life is going wrong. Why does God allow this? Why doesn't He help me?" Have you heard these types of remarks? Well, many feel this way. They think God is failing them. Is this true? No, of course not. God doesn't take off as soon as His children have tough hills to climb.

However, God's presence does not mean that you will experience prosperity, happiness and wealth always. He does not guarantee that you will never be faced with dangerous situations. God's Word promises that He will always be near. Call on Him. He will help you.

Even though you may feel like you are being led like a lamb to the slaughter and that life is knocking you down, know that you are never alone. The hands of God your Father enfold you. You are safe in His arms, even though you may be bleeding. He will dress your wounds with His Spirit and fill your life with hope and strength. He renews His true care of you every day. The sun of His righteousness will shine on you each day.

DAY 172

All You Need

"My grace is enough; it's all you need."
– 2 Corinthians 12:9 THE MESSAGE –

"It's mine!" Those are the words of a two-year-old if you dare take his toy. And if you don't return it promptly, there is war, because it's "mine!" Some adults also live in this manner. Everything in the shops, every new product, has their name on it. "Mine" is what they say to themselves when they see a new car, clothes, furniture, video camera, laptop or cell phone. There is no rest for their soul until that item has also become theirs. As soon as the item has been purchased, they want something else.

We live in a world which continuously creates one desire after the other. We never have enough things that can be regarded as "mine." If we don't guard against it, we can become prisoners of our desires. That is why John warns against a continuous desire for things that have to be exhibited on the "must-have" shelf (1 John).

As a believer, I often say that the Lord is my Shepherd. Well, then, I should have such a deep desire for His love and mercy that I make His love "mine" with everything that I have in me. Only then will I really have enough.

DAY 173

The Great Search

Because You are my helper, I sing for joy in the shadow of Your wings.

– Psalm 63:7 NLT –

Do you sometimes long for someone so badly that it feels as if you have chest pains? Do you know that deep yearning? If you do, you will have compassion with the writer of Psalm 63 who calls out to God. He longs and thirsts for God like someone in the desert who needs water urgently. Do you know this intense thirst for God? Do you start off every morning in the desert searching for Living Water? And at night, when you lie in bed, do you long for God's strong hand on your shoulder (v. 7)? Does your inner being constantly shout for God? Then be assured that God can be found by every sincere seeker. He will quench your thirst. He will satisfy your longing. He will meet you somewhere.

No one who sincerely calls for God does so in vain. No one who seeks His company walks away empty-handed. God lets Himself be found. He does not hide. He is not busy with other more important matters when you call on Him today. Seek and you will find! That is what the Man of Nazareth said. He knows the heart of His Father best of all.

Day 174

Precious Treasure

"Wherever your treasure is, there the desires of your heart will also be."

– Matthew 6:21 NLT –

Everything that glitters is not gold. Sometimes the most precious treasures are not buried deep under the ground, but can be found near the surface instead. Look around—your companion, your parents and your children are the Lord's special gifts to you. They are your most precious earthly possessions. The Lord does not want you to struggle through life alone. That is why He gave you your loved ones. They are your helpers, your towers of strength, your biggest supporters, and your gold. They are the ones who constantly pray, stand by you and carry you.

What are you doing for your loved ones? Do you pray for them regularly, too? Do you set an example for them in your commitment to the Lord? Do you set aside enough time for them? Or are you always tired when you have time to devote to them? Do you constantly have the excuse of some more work to finish or two more telephone calls to make? If so, you have not really discovered God's special treasures. You are looking for gold in all the wrong places.

Look at your loved ones once more. Thank God for them and live close to them.

Day 175

God's Way

The LORD directs the steps of the godly. He delights in every detail of their lives.

– Psalm 37:23 NLT –

Frank Sinatra sang, "I did it my way." One day I would like to sing, "I did it God's way." In fact, I want to sing it tonight, before I go to bed. I do not want to postpone my walk with God one more day. Days come and go! Opportunities abound, but sometimes days to walk with God only arrive once. There are more than enough wasted, unused days in my life. I want to stop wasting time in such a senseless way.

As Paul said in the letter to the Ephesians, I want to redeem my time. I will start by living and experiencing today (which I have received by the grace of God), in the right way. I can't afford to waste today. I want to welcome Jesus into my life today, as a special honored guest. Then I will use my time effectively.

I know that Jesus never waits until tomorrow or the next day to help. He sets His watch to the needs of broken people. His diary is overflowing with appointments with people who have sinned. That is where I want to be, with those people: radically flat-out, at top gear, at today's speed.

DAY 176

Keeping Silent

Joyful are those who have the God of Israel as their helper, whose hope is in the LORD their God.
– Psalm 146:5 NLT –

How can we possibly look the other way when 30,000 people die worldwide every day due to water pollution and the serious illnesses related to it? How can we remain silent when hundreds of people die every day due to cholera? Doesn't it deeply affect us when global warming is threatening the continued existence of our planet? Can we turn a blind eye when poisonous gases are warming our atmosphere beyond its limits? Can we remain deaf when racist language dominates many of the conversations around us? Dare we keep quiet when innocent blood is shed due to senseless crimes?

Should we keep on praying when everyone around us has thrown in the towel and started following their own leads? Should we also surrender and give up hope? No, how could we? The living Lord is with us, the One who says that those who cry and grieve about all the suffering will soon be comforted (Matt. 5). We can cry, but also laugh at the same time. Therefore, our hearts are heavily burdened, but also light. Because the Lord is also present in the darkness which sometimes threatens to overwhelm us.

Day 177

Focusing on Christ

Whatever is true, whatever is noble, whatever is right, whatever is pure, whatever is lovely, whatever is admirable—if anything is excellent or praiseworthy—think about such things.

– Philippians 4:8 NIV –

Your brain is the original energy saver. It constantly uses the experiences, emotions, and thought patterns from the past to dictate your behavior, emotions and feelings now. Your old thoughts can keep you captive for the rest of your life if you don't deliberately choose daily *what* and *how* you want to think. Therefore, Paul tells us in Ephesians 4 not to get stuck with weak minds that think sinful thoughts. He knows that our thought patterns can degenerate into useless, addictive routines.

In the same breath, the apostle Paul writes in 2 Corinthians 10 that we need to take our thoughts captive. Every one of them needs to be arrested in the powerful name of Christ. Those thoughts that fuel anger, suspicion, bitterness and immorality need to be unmasked and handed over to God. Such thoughts need to be identified, unmasked, and refused free access to our minds. Otherwise we can become prisoners of addictive thoughts and accompanying behavioral patterns. Renewed minds offer the key to a new understanding of Christ. Let's focus our thoughts on Christ and be free!

Day 178

Blind to Circumstance

God has said, "Never will I leave you; never will I forsake you."

– Hebrews 13:5 NIV –

One can so easily become blind to everything but one's own circumstances. Then it's easy to fall back on that old evergreen complaint: "The Lord has forsaken me." Listen, it is definitely not true. Your own feelings and circumstances should never be the yardstick against which you measure how far (or near) God is from you. Don't think that God is far away simply because you feel that it is the case. Don't let your troubles make you decide that He has forgotten you, because God will never forsake you in difficult times.

We allow our feelings to lead us by the nose far too easily. Whenever it feels as if the road to heaven is closed, we decide that God has given us up as a bad job. Yet the Bible tells us that not even dire circumstances can ever separate us from Him (Rom. 8:31-39).

God proved that we are extremely valuable when He sent His only Son to make us His permanent property. We are so important that God sent His Spirit to transform us into permanent dwellings for the Almighty.

Day 179

Our Awesome God

"My Father, who has given them to Me, is greater than all; no one can snatch them out of My Father's hand."

– John 10:29 NIV –

A few years ago my wife and I traveled through Turkey with a wonderful group of people, where one afternoon we experienced a solar eclipse. For a few minutes the moon moved across the sun and the world around us was pitch dark. Everybody who experienced it was overwhelmed, as was I. Once again I realized just how big and mighty God is. I was in awe over His power. He has the power to push the moon quietly across the path of the sun. He can extinguish the sun when it suits Him. But the tenderness with which He guards His creation so that the planets remain in orbit day after day is too much for me to understand.

Psalm 8 cries out, "What is man that You are mindful of him?" In the greater scheme of things we are a handful of nothings, little bits of dust in life's massive machine. Yet God concerns Himself with tiny human beings like us. He creates us out of dust and He lets us live in front of Him, daily. He even loves us. God holds us, Christ's sheep, lovingly in His hands (vv. 28-30). Praise His name!

Day 180

God Knows You

You hem me in behind and before, and You lay Your hand upon me.

– Psalm 139:5 NIV –

Never, ever think that you are an accident. Psalm 139:13-14 (NIV) exclaims, "For you created my inmost being; you knit me together in my mother's womb. I praise You because I am fearfully and wonderfully made; Your works are wonderful, I know that full well." God knows you inside out, from way back when. He knows more about you than you could ever know about yourself. Before your birth God already knew the path that your life would follow. "You know me inside and out, You know every bone in my body; You know exactly how I was made, bit by bit, how I was sculpted from nothing into something. Like an open book, You watched me grow from conception to birth; all the stages of my life were spread out before You, the days of my life all prepared before I'd even lived one day" (vv. 15-16 THE MESSAGE).

God knows every thought that crosses your mind. He sees your whole existence in a flash, in all its dimensions. There is no part of your life that you can hide from Him. All your decisions, dreams, fears, joys—literally every millimeter of your life—are known to God. He looks right through you. Don't try to understand how it works, because it isn't possible.

About the Author

Stephan Joubert is a renowned speaker, leadership consultant, pastor, and acclaimed author. He is an Extraordinary Professor in Theology at the University of the Free State and a research fellow in Theology at the Radboud University in Nijmegen, Netherlands. Stephan is also the editor of echurch, an online community of followers of Jesus, with more than 55 000 members worldwide. He is married to Marietjie and they have two married daughters.